CHRISTIAN ROMAN EMPIRE SERIES

Vol. 7

THE LIFE

OF

SAINT SIMEON STYLITES

*A TRANSLATION OF THE SYRIAC TEXT
IN BEDJAN'S* ACTA MARTYRUM ET
SANCTORUM, *VOL. IV*

Translated by

Rev. Frederick Lent, PhD

Evolution Publishing
Merchantville NJ
2009

Originally Published in
Journal of the American Oriental Society

Rev. Frederick Lent, PhD
*The Life of St. Simeon Stylites: A Translation of the Syriac Text
in Bedjan's Acta Martyrum et Sanctorum, Vol. IV*
JAOS, Volume 35, 1915, pp. 103–198

Also included in this volume:

Charles C. Torrey
The Letters of Simeon the Stylite
JAOS, Volume 20, 1899, pp. 253–276

ISBN 978-1-889758-91-6

Library of Congress Cataloging-in-Publication Data

The life of Saint Simeon Stylites : a translation of the Syriac text in Bedjan's
Acta martyrum et sanctorum, vol. IV / translated by Frederick Lent
    p. cm. -- (Christian Roman empire series ; 7)
 "Originally published in Journal of the American Oriental Society, 1915."
 Includes also another article from the Journal of the American Oriental Society,
entitled The Letters of Simeon the Stylite by Charles C. Torrey, originally
published in 1899.
 Includes bibliographical references and index.
 ISBN 978-1-889758-91-6
 1. Simeon Stylites, Saint, d. 459. 2. Christian saints--Syria--Biography. I. Lent,
Frederick. II. Bedjan, Paul, 1938–1920. Acta martyrum et sanctorum Syriace.
 BR1720.S52L54 2008
 270.2092--dc22
 [B]
                                    2008052614

TABLE OF CONTENTS
TO THE 2009 EDITION

PREFACE TO THE 2009 EDITION

Simeon the Stylite is one of those fascinating examples of early Christian monastic asceticism that seems so completely alien to the modern world. Far from seeking relief from even the smallest trials of everyday life, holy men like Simeon sought to amplify them in frightful and spectacular ways. In the literature of the time, such men were given epithets like athlete, warrior, and combatant. And indeed, in the spiritually charged life of the Christian Roman Empire, these holy champions attained heights of fame and glory every bit as lofty as those worldly heroes of earlier times.

Born at the end of the 4th century, Simeon was the prototype of the pillar saint. Not satisfied with the standard ascetic practices of the time which included long fasts, bodily mortification, confinement in small spaces, etc., Simeon felt called by God to do something truly radical and make his stand atop a high column sixty feet off the ground. For thirty-seven years he remained at his station between heaven and earth, exposed to the elements and suffering grievously for the greater glory of God. So famous an example did Simeon provide that after his death in AD 459, pillar saints sprung up all over the eastern empire. Only a single example may be found in the west—Saint Vulfolaic, a Lombard, who lived atop a pillar for a short time in northern Gaul.[1]

Simeon's superhuman feats of mortification and the miracles achieved through his intercession won him fame throughout the world. In a brief biography written while Simeon was still alive, the bishop and ecclesiastical historian Theodoret, who knew the saint personally, claimed that people from everywhere made pilgrimages to Simeon, from Arabs, Persians, and Armenians, to Spaniards, Britons, and Gauls. "He became so well known in the great city of Rome," says Theodoret, "that small portraits of him were set up on a column at the entrances of every shop."[2]

As a result of his fame, three *Vitae* of Mar Simeon have come down to us from antiquity, along with several letters purported to have been dictated by him. Of the three *Vitae*, two of them are quite brief—that of Theodoret mentioned above, and another written after his death by a certain Antonius who was a disciple of the holy man.[3] The third *Vita* is commonly called the Syriac Life by scholars, and it is a translation of that work which appears in this present volume.

The Syriac Life was most likely written by Simeon's disciples soon after his death. Called "a majestic, at times elegant work of hagiography" by Prof. Susan Ashbrook Harvey,[4] the Syriac Life is by far the longest and most detailed of the extant *Vitae*. It traces Simeon's journey as he is transformed from a simple peasant boy, into a champion of physical endurance, from an outcast monk despised by his jealous peers, into a paragon of holiness placed on par with Moses and Elijah.

This translation of the Syriac Life was originally executed by Reverend Frederick Lent, a Baptist minister and one time president of Elmira College. Lent's translation was first published in the *Journal of the American Oriental Society* in 1915, and is reprinted here with the permission of the Society. This edition reproduces Rev. Lent's translation faithfully, adding only a few innovations to make the text more accessible to general readers. Footnotes have been set as endnotes, additional paragraph markers have been inserted to break up large blocks of text, and chapter headings and titles have been added where logical. A few additional notes have been included as well to explain some of the more obscure terminology and to update obsolete references where possible.

This edition also includes another article from the *Journal of the American Oriental Society* entitled "The Letters of Simeon the Stylite" by Charles C. Torrey, originally published in 1899. It was decided to include this article because Rev. Lent refers to it several times in his text and it is still cited with some regularity by patristics scholars. This article translates several contradictory letters which were purportedly dictated by Saint Simeon and also contains a useful discussion of the holy man's opinion of the Council of Chalcedon—an opinion which appears to have been manipulated after his death for polemical reasons.

—Anthony P. Schiavo, Jr.
Merchantville, NJ
December 2008

NOTES

1. See Gregory of Tours, *The History of the Franks*, pp. 446–447.
2. Doran, p. 75.
3. Translations of these two *Vitae*, along with a translation of a different recension of the Syriac Life may be found in Doran, *The Lives of Simeon Stylites* (1992).
4. *Vigiliae Christianae*, vol. 42, no. 4, p. 381.

2009 EDITION BIBLIOGRAPHY AND FURTHER READING

Assemani, Giuseppi Simone 2002 [1719–1728]. *Bibliotheca Orientalis Clementino-Vaticana.* Gorgias Press: Piscataway, NJ.

Assemani, Stephanus Evodius 1972 [1748]. *Acta Sanctorum Martyrum Orientalium et Occidentalium.* Gregg International Publishing: Westmead, UK

Atchley, E. G. Cuthbert F. 1909. *A History of the Use of Incense in Divine Worship.* Longmans, Green and Co.: London.

Bedjan, P. 2007 [1890–1897] *Acts of Martyrs and Saints: Acta Martyrum et Sanctorum.* Gorgias Press: Piscataway, NJ.

Bury, J. B. 1958 [1923]. *History of the Later Roman Empire: From the Death of Theodosius I to the Death of Justinian.* Vols. I and II. Dover Publications: Mineola, NY.

Cotelerius, Jean Baptiste 1677. *Ecclesiae Graecae Monumenta.* Muguet: Paris.

Cowper, B. Harris 1864. "Selections from the Syriac: No. 1—The Chronicle of Edessa." *Journal of Sacred Literature and Biblical Record.* Williams & Norgate: London.

Doran, Robert (transl.) 1992. *The Lives of Simeon Stylites.* Cistercian Publications: Kalamazoo, MI.

Evagrius. Edward Walford (transl.) 2008 [1846]. *The Ecclesiastical History of Evagrius.* Evolution Publishing, Merchantville, NJ.

Ferguson, Everett et al. (eds.) 1998. *Encyclopedia of Early Christianity.* Garland Publishing: New York.

Graetz, Heinrich. Bella Löwy (transl.) 1892. *History of the Jews.* David Nutt: London.

Gregory of Tours. Lewis Thorpe (transl.) 1977. *The History of the Franks.* Penguin Books: London.

Harduin, J. 1714. *Acta Conciliorum*, vol. ii. Paris.

Harnack, Adolph. Neil Buchanan (transl.) 1895. *History of Dogma.* Williams & Norgate: London.

Harvey, S. Ashbrook 1988. "The Sense of a Stylite: Perspectives on Simeon the Elder." *Vigiliae Christianae*, Vol. 42, No. 4.

Herbermann, Charles G., et al. 1913. *The Catholic Encyclopedia: An International Work of Reference on the Constitution, Doctrine, Discipline, and History of the Catholic Church.* The Encyclopedia

Press: New York. Electronic edition available online at http://www.newadvent.org/cathen/

Land, J.P.N. 1862. *Anecdota Syriaca.* Leiden.

Lucian. J. L. Lightfoot (ed.) 2003. *On the Syrian Goddess.* Oxford University Press: Oxford.

Migne, J.-P. (ed.) 1857–1866. *Patrologia Graeca.* Vols. 1–85. Paris.

Neander, Johann Augustus. Joseph Torrey (transl.) 1858. *General History of the Christian Religion and Church.* Henry G. Bohn: London.

Nöldeke, Theodor. James A. Crichton (transl.) 2001 [1904]. *Compendious Syriac Grammar.* Eisenbrauns: Winona Lake, IN.

Nöldeke, Theodor. John Sutherland Black (transl.) 1892. *Sketches from Eastern History.* Adam & Charles Black: London & Edinburgh.

Parise, Frank 2002. *The Book of Calendars: Conversion Tables for Ancient, African, Near Eastern, Indian, Asian, Central American and Western Calendars.* Gorgias Press: : Piscataway, NJ.

Pharr, C. (transl.) 1952. *The Theodosian Code and Novels and the Sirmondian Constitutions.* Princeton University Press: Princeton, NJ.

Theophanes. Roger Scott (transl.) 1997. *The Chronicle of Theophanes Confessor. Oxford University Press.* Oxford.

Trombley, Frank R. and John W. Watt (eds.) 2000. *The Chronicle of Pseudo-Joshua the Stylite.* Liverpool University Press: Liverpool, UK.

Wright, William 2001 [1894]. *A Short History of Syriac Literature.* Gorgias Press: Piscataway, NJ.

INTRODUCTION

This famous saint was born near the close of the fourth century at Ṣīṣ, near Nicopolis, in Northern Syria. Long before Simeon lived, there had been at the sanctuary of the goddess Attar'athe, in Hierapolis, a tall pillar, on which a man stood seven days twice a year for communion with the gods (Lucian, *De Dea Syria,* c. 28 sq.). But, as Nöldeke points out (*Sketches from Eastern History*, Trans. London 1892, ch. VII), Simeon probably had never heard of it; the practice had died out long before he was born. Theodoret, an educated Syrian, regarded Simeon as the father of all who adopted life upon pillars. Besides the sketch of Simeon's career given by Theodoret, (see Migne, *Patrologia Graeca*, v. 82, Theodoretus 3), the historian Evagrius gives a short notice of his life. Another Greek biography, said to be written by Anthony, a disciple of Simeon, Nöldeke refers to a late date, on account of its extravagances.

The Syriac biography with which we are concerned was probably written shortly after Simeon's death, which occurred in 459 AD. There are three known manuscripts of this Syriac Life. The Vatican MS. was published by S. E. Assemani, *Acta Sanctorum Martyrum* (Rome, 1748), Vol. II, pp. 273–394. The two other MSS. are in the British Museum. Bedjan, in preparing the Life of Simeon for publication in his *Acta Martyrum et Sanctorum*, first copied the text of Assemani. Then he collated it with the MS. B. M. Add. 12174, and so discovered that this text not only gave the facts in a different order, but contained material not found in Assemani's text. As one or two leaves of this MS. are lacking, he made use of another still older,

Add. 14484, which gave the same facts in the same order as 12174, but more soberly and concisely. Because of its simple, beautiful style, and because of its order of events, which appears more logical than that of Assemani's edition, Bedjan regarded the text of this MS. 14484 as the oldest of the three. One important passage (p. 643), containing a very friendly allusion to the Emperor Leo, but altered in Assemani's text by the erasure of the eulogistic words (p. 393), caused Bedjan to conclude that this MS. was written before Monothelitism invaded Syria, that is, before the seventh century AD. It is the text of this MS., B. M. Add. 14484, which is given in Bedjan's *Acta*, vol. IV, pp. 507–644, and which is here translated. (See Bedjan, *Acta Martyrum et Sanctorum*, Leipzig, 1894; vol. IV, Preface pp. XI–XIV.)

What relation does the version represented in Assemani's text bear to that given by Bedjan?[1] The two texts, when they report the same incident, use practically the same words. The variations in language are, however, too numerous to mention. One text may employ a synonym for the term used in the other, or a whole sentence may occur in one which is not in the other, or a scripture quotation may be peculiar to one text. But in spite of these differences, the wording is substantially the same in the two texts. The differences, however, are sufficiently numerous and striking to show that neither text was copied from the other. Furthermore, the differences between Bedjan's and Assemani's texts exclude the possibility that both could have been derived from one common MS. We have here two quite independent recensions, as is shown by the variation in the order of events narrated. If we number the paragraphs in Bedjan's text, beginning with page 532, consecutively, and then attach the same numbers to the same incidents as given in Assemani's text, the order in the latter is as follows: 31–57, 21–30, 32,

2–11, 58, 59, 61, 62, 64, 66. This shows how differently the same material is grouped in the two texts, and makes it evident that they represent different recensions, neither one derived from the other. This opinion is strengthened by the presence of the material found in Bedjan's text which is not in the other.

This matter peculiar to Bedjan's text is found in seven Sections. The first is p. 507 from the beginning to p. 508, l. 5. This opening paragraph is simple and natural, written in the usual manner of introduction to the life of a famous man. It is extremely unlikely that an author presenting for the first time an account of the Saint's career would begin as abruptly, as Assemani's text does, without a single reference to the readers for whom it was intended. That the biographer had such readers in mind is shown later (e.g. on p. 548, Bedjan; Assemani, parallel passage) by a direct address to them. The fuller text is probably the more original in this instance.

The second section, Bedjan, p. 512, l. 14–p. 514, l. 17, is an account of a raid made by Isaurian bandits who took captive some people of Ṣīṣ, Simeon's native village. The Saint was instrumental in delivering the captives, whom he rescued by miraculously paralyzing the arm of the robber chief. He also procured water by miracle. There is no reference in the context to make the inclusion of the story necessary, Assemani reads smoothly omitting it. On the other hand such a raid was probable, and the account is sober and quite in keeping with the context. There is nothing to render it suspicious, or to mark it as a later addition. No motive is apparent for its introduction, if it did not stand in the original account.

Section three, Bedjan, p. 520, l. 3–p. 521, l. 11 (see Assemani, p. 28, l. 12) tells how, when other monks had finished the nocturns and gone to rest, Simeon would stand weighed down with a stone hung to his neck, keeping vigil. When it was time for the others to arise, he would remove the stone and join in the prescribed service. One night, as he was putting the stone on his neck, he fell asleep. Deeply chagrined at thus yielding to what he regarded as Satanic temptation, he procured a rounded piece of wood, on which he stood thereafter during the nightly vigil, in order that, if he should fall asleep, the wood, rolling, might awaken him. These severe practices aroused the hostility of the monks, who would have him to do only as the rules enjoined. Now, although Assemani does not have this section, his text does have the story of the rounded piece of wood, given in another connection where it is quite irrelevant. After Bedjan, p. 521, 5th line from the bottom, Assemani (p. 280) inserts this paragraph:

> "The manner in which the monks afflicted him, and harassed him, in order that he should conform to their mode of life, is beyond description. For many times they assembled and said to the abbot, 'If he will not conform to the same mode of life as the brethren, let him leave the monastery! But the abbot did not act on their protest, because he loved Simeon greatly, since he saw his labor and toil, and knew that envy prompted them to say, 'Let him conform to our mode of life.' For by night Simeon made a piece of wood round, and stood on it," etc.

Then follows material, part of which is found earlier in Bedjan. It can hardly be doubted that Bedjan's account is here the more original. The section is orderly and natural, while the other text has introduced in a disjointed manner the one item it preserves. In this instance, again, the longer text is the preferable.

The fourth section is found in Bedjan, p. 525, 1. 15–p.

526, l. 5. By comparison with Assemani (p. 185) it will be seen that the latter gives a different account of Simeon's exit from the monastery, and the context does not require for smooth reading the material given in Bedjan, although Assemani's text omits the motive for the prayer it records, viz. "If it is Thy will that I perform the Lenten fast in this place, direct me." Bedjan's text gives this, by stating in exact chronology that the time was just before Lent, in the year 458 of the Antiochan Era.[2] The entrance into the monastery at this time marked an important crisis in Simeon's life. That a careful and intimate biographer should preserve the date of this entrance into Telneshē, is therefore just what we should expect. The account contains no exaggeration, but just a simple story of faith and divine guidance, which suggests no motive for its arbitrary insertion by a later hand. Here again, therefore, the longer account may be regarded as original and preferable.

The fifth section, Bedjan, p. 538, l. 19–p. 539, l. 3, contains a brief description of the Saint's clothing, together with a general statement that he glorified God. The absence of this paragraph in Assemani's text does not mar the story, but its presence in Bedjan's text gives vividness to the account, and it is reasonable to suppose that his biographer would have mentioned just such a fact as is here recorded. The failure to do so is against the originality of Assemani's text.

The sixth section is the longest one peculiar to Bedjan's, text, extending from p. 548, l. 21 to p. 555, l. 2. It contains a descriptive resume of Simeon's monastic life from the day he entered upon the practice of standing on a stone in the mandra, and began to immure himself during the Lenten fast. Then follow stories of various miracles of healing. The section is fittingly introduced by a general eulogy on Simeon's healing powers, and a direct address to the reader, with a promise to give an account of some things selected from many, sufficient to illustrate the Saint's miraculous activity. The section is followed by further similarly illustrating material, which would seem out of place if this section were omitted. In Bedjan's text, the reason for the introduction of any incident is always clear. Stories which illustrate a phase of Simeon's life are grouped together. Assemani's text, on the contrary, is disjointed, and shows no such orderly and logical arrangement. The general scheme of the life as given in Bedjan seems to demand that this section should be given here.

The last section, Bedjan, p. 643, l. 15–p. 644, l. 12, is the closing paragraph of the life. All it records was evidently known to the writer of MS. B. M. Add. 12174 (see Bedjan, p. 643, Note), and its absence gives a very abrupt termination to Assemani's text. Evagrius was evidently familiar with this longer ending paragraph, and it seems more natural than Assemani's version. On the expunging of the words applied to Leo, (Bedjan, p. 643, Assemani, p. 393) Assemani has this note (p. 412, Note 47):

"Haec iisdem plane verbis leguntur apud Evagrium lib. 1, cap. 13, pag. 271. Leonis autem Imperatoris nomen ex codice nostro expunctum est, fol. 77, colum. 1, l. 17, a quonam vel quo concilio, nescio Suspicior, nebulonem quemdam Jacobitam in odium Catholici hujus Imperatoris, qui Chalcedonense Concilium acerrime propugnavit, ejus nomen abrasisse. "

There is nothing in Bedjan's closing paragraph to mark it as anything but the original. Thus a comparison of the whole text of Bedjan with that of Assemani leads us to regard the former as in every respect the superior and earlier version. If a later editor added the paragraphs which are peculiar to the longer version, we might expect to find some differences of vocabulary and idiom in the added paragraphs. But Bedjan's text is a unit in point of style, and as we have seen, the verbal agreement with the shorter life in the narration of the same incidents is very marked. Some readings in Bedjan's text are obviously preferable: e.g., "Timothy, the disciple of Paul,"[3] where the other text reads, "disciple of Simeon." Assemani's text betrays its author's distance from the age of Simeon, e.g., "As said his acquaintances and those familiar with him from his youth" (p. 269, l. 16, 17; cf. Bedjan, p. 508, last line), but Bedjan's text never hints at any dependence upon hearsay. It is consistent with the statement, more than once repeated, that the writer or writers learned directly from Simeon the facts of his life not immediately known by observation.

Bedjan is right in thinking that the more logical order found in his text points to the original composition, and not to editorial work. As we have indicated, Bedjan's version is orderly in its groupings of material. Both Assemani's and Bedjan's versions agree, in the main, in the narration of the story of Simeon's early life. But when once he has begun his monastic career, and all that follows is descriptive of his mode of life and illustrative of his activities, as ascetic and miracle worker, as prophet and beholder of visions, Bedjan's material is logically arranged, every incident finding its proper place under an appropriate heading. For example, if the announcement is made, "Now concerning the visions which Simeon saw," all the material introduced is relevant. In Assemani's text, on the contrary, no such order is observed, as may be readily seen by a glance at the numbers which show the different placing of the same incidents in the two recensions. It can scarcely be doubted that the logical arrangement is more original than the haphazard and disjointed method followed in the shorter version.

Of the two recensions, then, Bedjan's text represents the original story, and that of Assemani a later and shorter version.

As we have noticed, the shorter recension has omitted nothing which is vitally important in giving a correct impression of the saint's life. We gain the same view of his career and estimate of his personality in the shorter as in the longer account. Probably the omitted material was purposely left out by an early editor. In one instance, at least, he composed a paragraph, substituting it for the omitted section, in order to give a motive for what followed (p. 280, Assemani, explains that the envy of the monks led to persecution, see above, p. 105f.). The opening and closing paragraphs of the longer recension add nothing to the story. The man who undertook the copy did not have the same interest in his readers that the original author had. His attention is riveted to Simeon's career, so he passes at once to the narrative. Being further removed from the age of the saint than the author, he can not feel, as the author did, when he lovingly penned the closing sentences, that Simeon's influence and prayers still brood over the whole creation. So the copyist omitted this, to him, unnecessary paragraph. None of the material peculiar to the longer recension adds to our knowledge of Simeon. It could be left out without seriously damaging the narrative.

A later writer who was well acquainted with this abridged life, but having no text before him, wrote as he remembered, and gave us the story as it stands in Assemani's text. Memory could not preserve the logical orderly arrangement of the original story, but could hold nearly every incident and almost keep the writer to a literal reproduction of the history. Some things he could recall without remembering the exact connection, as, for example, the story of Simeon's vigils kept by standing on a piece of rounded wood. This impressed him as a meritorious act, and was mentioned, while he forgot that the saint was led to adopt the practice because he fell asleep one night while tying the stone weight to his neck. So, too, he remembered that Simeon entered the monastery of Telneshē, but he forgot the year and the exact season. The fact was for him more important than the connection.

There is no improbability inherent in the supposition that a man could write thus from memory. Parallels not a few may be found in all literatures, and particularly among the Orientals of the first Christian centuries, when memory was more tenacious than in an age of many books. Even in modern times, Arab writers can tell with astonishing verbal exactness, from memory, stories much longer than that of Simeon the Stylite. In Codex Vaticanus Clx. the Life of Simeon is followed by a letter from the Elder, Cosmas, to Simeon. To the letter is appended a colophon (*Acta Martyrum*, Assemani, II. 394ff. copied in Bedjan, *Acta Martyrum et Sanctorum* IV. 648f.), in which we read "May God and his Christ remember for good Simeon bar Apollon, and Bar Ḥaṭar the son of 'Udan, who assumed the labor of making this book, "The Glorious Deeds of Mar Simeon the Blessed." They made it by the toil of their hands and the sweat of their brows. — — — This book was finished in the month of Nisan, on the 17th of the month, on the fourth day of the week, in the year five hundred and twenty-one, of the Antiochian chronology. — — — And let everyone who reads it pray for those who undertook the work and made this book, that God may give them everlasting forgiveness of sins. Amen and Amen.

Let everyone who reads and makes, pray for him who wrote. — — — Farewell in our Lord; and pray for me."

Assemani thought that Cosmas composed the life of Simeon, and that the date here given (521 of the Antiochan reckoning = 473 AD) was that of the transcription of this MS; he regarded Simeon bar Apollon and Bar Ḥaṭar as those who requested, or aided in, the writing of the life. Wright thought they were the paid copyists of this portion of Codex Vat. Clx. Nöldeke (*Sketches*, etc., p. 225), Bedjan (*Acta Mart.* IX, p. xiii), Torrey (*Letters of Simeon*, p. 274f.), and Duval (*La Lit. Syriaque*, p. 160) regard these two men as the original authors, and 473 AD as the date of the composition of the Life.[4]

It seems to the present writer more probable that the names given in this colophon are those of the men who reproduced the abridged Life from memory, "by the toil of their hands and the sweat of their brows." It is much more difficult to suppose that the colophon contains matter which stood originally at the end of the longer Life, but which has been lost from there. As it stands in the Vatican Codex, it is a whole, and evidently in its original place. It was added to the MS. containing the abridged life and the letter of Cosmas. Therefore, 473 AD is the date when the text of Codex Vat. Clx. was written from memory by these two men, Simeon bar Apollon, and Bar Ḥaṭar, son of 'Udan. The original Life, composed by one of Simeon's disciples, was accordingly written between the Saint's death, in 459 AD and 473 AD, when the two men made their memory recension of the abridged story. Bedjan's "Life" was probably written shortly after 459 AD. The MS. B. M. Add. 14484 is written on parchment in the Estrangelo character, and was dated by Wright as of the sixth century.

The text of this Syriac composition is a model of its kind. Nöldeke has cited Assemani's edition more than two hundred times in his grammar, in illustrating classical Syriac usage (see Nöldeke, *Compendious Syriac Grammar*, Trans. Crichton, London, 1904, p. 333). Thus will be seen the importance of the text for the student of Syriac. Of no less interest to the general student, we trust, will prove this "Life of Simeon the Stylite," here translated into English for the first time.

NOTES

1 See the article by C. C. Torrey, *The Letters of Simeon the Stylite*, published in the *Journal of the American Oriental Society*, vol. XX (1899), pp. 253–276. Professor Torrey maintained that the Bedjan recension is the original, and pointed out (pp. 275 f.) one passage in which it is certain that the text of Assemani is merely an abridgment. The proof needs to be considerably extended, however, and an attempt to do this is made in the following text. *Note to the 2009 edition*: Torrey's article is included as part of this present volume. See p. 115 ff.

2. *Note to the 2009 edition:* 458 of the Antiochene era = AD 410.

3. See Bedjan, *Acta Martyrum et Sanctorum*, page 511.

4. *Note to the 2009 edition:* For additional discussion of the authorship of Bedjan's Life, see Doran, *The Lives of Simeon Stylites*, p. 44 ff.

TABLE OF CONTENTS

THE HEROIC DEEDS OF
MAR SIMEON
THE CHIEF OF THE ANCHORITES

PREFACE

To our brethren and sons and friends, children of the Holy
Catholic Church: we make known to you in our writings
the glorious deeds of the Man of God, who was a friend to
the Christ. He gave himself to service in the vineyard of our
Lord from the dawn even until the evening all the days of
his life. He turned the stubborn of heart to conviction, and
finished his struggle with praise, and his Lord took him to
himself, that he might pay him the good reward of his labor
in the land of the consummation of life eternal—the blessed
Mar Simeon.

CHAPTER I
SIMEON'S ORIGINS AND EARLY LIFE

This glorious man, then, came from the region of Nicopolis,
and the name of his town was Şīş. Now he had Christian
parents who gave him baptism when he was small. He had
a brother whose name was Mar Shemshi, and they alone
remained to their parents of the many children whom
they had had. This blessed one from his boyhood loved to
shepherd the flocks of his parents, and he practiced himself
in toil, weariness and exhaustion. When he was grown up,

he had this peculiarity, that with much diligent care he used to collect storax[1] as he shepherded the flocks, and he would kindle a fire and burn the storax as incense, although he did not know just why he offered it. For hitherto the Scriptures had not been heard by him, and he was not persuaded in the fear of the Lord, while he was growing up from his boyhood among the flocks. He was radiant of countenance, and fair of face, and gentle and benevolent. In stature he was small, but in strength lusty, and in his running he was swift; and he won favor with everybody. He rejected food for himself while he fed others.

When his parents departed from this world, and he and his brother remained heirs, he entered the church, and heard as the epistle was read. And he asked those who stood with him: "These Scriptures, what are they? and what is in them?"

They said to him, "These are the Scriptures of God, who dwells in heaven; and the word of God is in them."

Then he felt much surprise in his heart, and on the following Sabbath he again entered the church, and heard those holy Scriptures with discernment. From that day on a surpassing diligence was his, and he gathered storax, and bought also that which his fellow-shepherds gathered, and with discernment placed it before our Lord, saying, "Let the sweet odor go up to God who is in heaven."

And after a few days, there appeared to the Blessed One a visitor as he was with the sheep. This was the first vision which he saw. For he saw that there came a man who stood by him, whose appearance was like lightning, his garments shining as the sun, and his face like rays of fire. He held a golden staff in his hand, and called and raised him up. When the Blessed One raised his eyes and saw this wonderful sign, he trembled and was affrighted, and fell upon his face on the ground. But he gave him his hand and, raising him up, said to him, "Be not afraid, but come after me without fear, for I have something to tell thee and shew thee. For the Lord wills that through thy hand His Name should be glorified. And thou shalt be chief and director and leader to his people, and to the sheep of his pasture, and by thy hand shall be established the laws and the commandments of the Holy Church. And many thou shalt turn from error to knowledge of the truth. And if thou dost serve acceptably, thy name shall be great among the Gentiles and even to the end of the earth, and kings and judges shall obey thee and thy commands. Only have patience and endurance, and let love be in thee toward all men. If thou dost indeed observe these things, not among the first and not among the last shall he be who glorifies himself and becomes as great as thou art."

Then afterwards he took him, and, going up to the mountain, placed him on its top and showed him stones which were lying there. And he said to him, "Take, and build!"

Said the Blessed One to him, "I do not know how to build, for I have never constructed any building."

He said to him, "Stand by and I will teach thee to build." Then he brought a stone which was carved and was very beautiful, and put it in the hands of Mar Simeon, and said to him, "Place it firmly at the east, and another on the north, and toward the south another, then place one upon them, and the building will be completed."

Said to him the Blessed One: "My Lord, what is this?"

The man replied, "This is an altar of that God whom thou dost worship, and to whom thou dost offer incense, and whose Scriptures thou hast heard."

Then he lead him from there, and said to him, "Come after me," and he took him into a martyrium which was near there, in which was laid Mar Timotheus the disciple of the apostle Paul. And when he was about to enter it, he saw before the court of the temple people, who could by no means be numbered; and they were clothed in white, and were like to bridegrooms. From the north also some in likeness of women clothed in purple, both modest and adorned with great beauty.

The Blessed One asked him, saying "My Lord, who are these?"

And he returned answer and said to him, "These men and women whom thou seest, these are they who are destined to receive at thy hands the Sign[2] of the Messiah, and be turned to the knowledge of the truth." Then he showed him also birds in the form of peacocks whose appearance was like the flame of fire. From their eyes went forth as it were swift lightnings. And when they saw the Blessed One, they unfolded their wings, and raised their heads and uttered a cry loud and strong, so that the earth trembled from their voice. Then the man motioned quietly and gently with the staff which was in his hand and made them be still.

Again he led the Blessed One and brought him within the temple; and when they had reached the altar and stood that they might pray, there went up from beneath the altar a man of pleasant mien whose appearance was more comely than the sun. His beauty was beyond compare, his face was glad and his countenance exceedingly cheerful. His hair was sprinkled with white and grew in clusters. And his garments were white, and his speech was soft and pleasant. And approaching, he greeted the Blessed Mar Simeon three times with much love, and said to him, "Blessed art thou, Simeon, if thou art equal to the part and service to which thou art called."

Then the two of them laid hold of him and brought him to the altar, and he[3] put in the mouth of Mar Simeon something white like snow and round like a pearl, and thus

4

he said: "Such a taste and such sweetness can not be found in the world." And his soul was satisfied and fat exceedingly. Then this man gave him the golden staff which he held, and said to him, "With this staff thou art to shepherd the flock of Christ. Be strong and mighty."

And when he had said these things to him, he became invisible and ascended.

CHAPTER II

SIMEON ESCAPES FROM ISAURIAN RAIDERS AND REDEEMS HIS NEPHEW FROM THEM

And after a while the Isaurians made a raid, and they came and entered Şīş, the native village of the Blessed One, which was in the region of Nicopolis, and the saint happened to be there. And they lifted up their hands, the Isaurians, against him, and took him. But the Lord delivered him from their hands. And they took many people captive, with Thomas, the son of the brother of the Blessed One, who also had departed from this world with a good name after living as an ascetic.

Then the Blessed One arose and went after those who were taken captive, and he found them in Kastelēn, encamping. And when the sentinels of the camp saw him, they seized him with watchful care, and led him to their chiefs, of whom the name of one was Bos and of the other Altamdora. They said to him, "Why is it thou hast been so rash as to come hither? And thou hast not feared, and thy heart hast not trembled?"

And he turned and said, "For the redemption of Thomas, my brother's son, and of this captivity have I come."

And when they saw, they were filled with anger, and gave order that they should take off his head with the sword. One of them then drew a dagger that he might smite him,

5

when immediately his right hand cleaved to his shoulder. And when they saw, fear fell upon them, and Bos their chief commanded that they should set out for another place. And when the Blessed One saw that they did not receive his supplication, he became incensed, and lifted up his hand against Bos, when immediately an unclean spirit took possession of him, and before the Blessed One he was convulsed, while he cried out and said, "Alas! thou servant of Jesus Christ."

When the Isaurians saw this phenomenon they were exceedingly affrighted, and they approached the Saint and said to him, "Tell us in truth if thou art the servant of God."

He said to them, "I am a Christian."

Then the Isaurian chief, as he stood in misery, said to the Blessed One, "My sins were stirred up against me in thy coming to me. But I beseech thee, offer up petition in my behalf."

The Blessed One said, "If indeed thou askest that I should offer petition on thy behalf, deliver into my hands this captivity which thou hast taken captive. For lo, their crying has gone up before God. And this trial He sent upon thee." Now this captivity was in number, men and women, four hundred. Then the Isaurian chief besought him that he would pray for him, and he would give the captivity into his hands. So the saint kneeled down and prayed. And when he finished his prayer, he stretched out to him his right hand and said to him, "In the name of the Lord Jesus Christ be healed." And immediately the unclean spirit departed from the man, and he was recovered, and he delivered all the captivity into the hands of the Blessed One. And the Blessed One, on his part, as he lead away all the captivity, commanded them that they should tell no one anything of what Christ had performed through his hands, for the deliverance of their lives; and he dismissed every one to his own country in peace.

While he was travelling on the mountain, he and Thomas, the son of his brother, his nephew thirsted for water. And the Blessed One lifted up his eyes, and prayed saying, "Oh Christ, who redeemed him from captivity, do not let him die of thirst." And at once water burst forth in the dry place, and they drank. And when their thirst was quenched, the water was sought but could not be found. And he led the youth and brought him to the village of the house of his kinsfolk.

CHAPTER III

A GIRL WHO PLAYS FALSE WITH SIMEON IS EXPOSED BY GOD

After these things the saint was in a fast twenty-one days, while he neither ate nor drank, a man who from his youth with food of flesh and drink of wine had been nourished. After those days he desired to eat. Now there was there in the village a certain man, a fisherman, and that very night he had caught fish, not a few. He had a daughter whose name was Mary, and her father left the fish with her and went away. And when the Blessed One came, he desired that she should give him three pounds, and take the price for it. But she denied with an oath, saying, "My father has not brought anything today." And when he went away from her, he stood with some soldiers who were on guard there because of the Isaurians, and with some of his townspeople. And as they were standing and talking, on a sudden something entered the girl and the fish and carried them out to the street before all the people; the girl herself leaping and gnashing her teeth and smiting her head and crying out at the Blessed Mar Simeon, while the fish also were leaping toward him.

7

And when the soldiers and the citizens saw this sign, they feared, and desired to gather the fish or calm the girl who was acting in such a shameful manner. But they could not. Then her father came, and many of her people, and they besought the Blessed One, and he went and took hold of her, and immediately she became quiet, and the fish also became still.

The saint said to her, "Because thou didst lie, God hath exposed thee publicly."

Those things did our Lord by the hands of the Blessed One, and he thoroughly fulfilled his petition, because it was not in gluttony he asked. For as he went out from there to the flock, as he wandered along on the mountain, he found a large fish, and having made the sign of the cross, he took it and went back to the village. When those soldiers who had been standing in the village saw it, they marvelled. And our Lord did also here a miracle. For for three days those soldiers and his fellow townsmen ate of it, and scarcely then was it consumed, because the blessing of the Lord rested upon it. Two of the soldiers who were there loved the Blessed One ardently, whose names were Selwāna and Bar Shabbatha. And until he stood upon the pillar, they came and went in his presence and narrated many things before him and his disciples.

CHAPTER IV
SIMEON DISPOSES OF HIS WORLDLY GOODS AND BEGINS HIS MONASTIC LIFE

The Blessed One was constant in fasting and prayer, entering the church among the first and going out among the last, while the greater part of the time he was passing the nights in the church. And from dawn until dark he was on his knees, and from dark till dawn he was standing in prayer. And when he was many times in these exercises, those who were of the same age as he were watching him, that they might see if he moved his feet, and changed from the spot in which he stood. But no one could find this in his case.

He had a brother whose name was Mar Shemshi, and it was his wish to have the inheritance divided with him. He said to him, "Do as you please, and whatever you want, appropriate without controversy." But his brother on his part divided everything rightly. For they had a paternal aunt, who was extremely rich. And in those days she departed from the world, and everything that she owned she left to the Blessed One. And everything she left he administered in the fear of God and gave to the poor and the needy; and especially he provided for the monastery of the Blessed Mar Eusebona, because the son of his paternal uncle was there, a man set for a sign, who was in the monastery thirty-five years. And from the time he entered the door of the monastery he had not turned back to see it.[4] And the Blessed One remembered that he had gone to that convent.

After these things he remained four months, because he had seed sown, and because he had many affairs to attend to in other convents and with the poor. But in all the fast of the forty days, while he was living in the city, he tasted no food except the Eucharist which he received when he was half way through the fast. And he waited until the great day. Also, again, in the matter of his seed which he had sown, our Lord did a great miracle. For he allowed the gleaners and the poor among the sheaves, and said to them, "Let everybody take as much as he can carry." And our Lord sent a blessing upon it, and there came forth sixty-fold and a hundred-fold. And bread also and boiled food he took out to the reapers. From it he set in order before the gleaners and before the poor, and they ate and were satisfied. And he with his own hands served them, and mixed the wine for

9

them. And these things the Blessed One told not in pride, but confessing and praising God for his providence towards him, repeating that which the apostle said, that "The gift of God is greater than can be told."

After these things he loaded whatever he had on camels, and took it to the convent of Mar Eusebona, and from it distributed in the other convents. And when he had been in the convent of Mar Eusebona three days, it happened that there came there Mar Mara, bishop of Gabola, a notable man. And the head of the convent brought him and presented him to him that he might be blessed by him. And when he saw the Blessed One, how fair of face and comely of visage he was, he marvelled at him and was astonished.

His brother also, Mar Shemshi, came to Mar Mara that he might be blessed by him. And when he saw him he said to him, "See, my son, that thy brother, who is younger than thou, hath chosen for himself that good part to which nothing is equal." And when Mar Shemshi heard his words, he also determined to become a monk. So he blessed them, and they two took the tonsure together. And they became choice vessels suitable for the use of their Lord, and finished their days in good reputation and in the service of righteousness.

And when he went away from him, this Mar Mara, the bishop, said to the abbot and to those who stood by him, "Truly, this blessed one, if the brethren permit him, will become a chosen vessel acceptable to God, and his fame will go out from one end of the earth to the other. For I know what sign I have seen in him."

And when Shemshi his brother had been with him about, five months, he also went and distributed whatever he owned to the poor, and to the convents. And whatever was left over he loaded on beasts of burden and brought to the convent where he was a novice.

CHAPTER V

THE ASCETIC PRACTICES OF MAR SIMEON; THE JEALOUSY OF HIS FELLOW MONKS

The Blessed Mar Simeon had no care for anything except how he might please his Lord. And when he had been with the monks a long time, he separated from them and went and digged for himself a hole in a corner of the garden up to his breast, and he stood in it two years in the oppressive heat of summer and the severe cold of winter. When the monks saw his hard toil, and no one of them was able to vie with him in his ascetic practices, they were filled with jealousy, and said to the abbot, "If he is not placed on an equality with us, he can not live here."

When the abbot saw the will of the monks, he entreated him either to mingle with the brothers or to diminish his toil; but he did not obey. Then the abbot said to them, "My sons, what should impel us to be hinderers to him who is constraining himself for our Lord's sake?"

One of the brothers thought that in hypocrisy he stood in that place, and wished to test him. So he came and stood above him, but in that very hour the justice of the Lord thrust him down and he fell and became dumb. The brothers who happened to be there ran and carried him and came and put him under a certain tree; and he vomited blood, and after three days died.

His practice while he was with the brotherhood was thus: from Sunday to Sunday[5] he took for himself some soaked lentils, but sometimes once in two weeks, or even once in three, while he constrained himself with severe effort. And when they forced him to sit at the refectory table, he gave himself the appearance of taking the food, although in reality he ate nothing at all. For the blessed

11

morsel which he received with the other brothers from the abbot he placed under the cover of his couch, and without his intent the brothers found it.

Again, when the brothers finished the nocturns and lay down to rest, he would hang a stone about his neck all the time that his companions were resting. When it was time for them to arise, he untied the stone from his neck, and stood with them for the service. But on one of the nights, when he had put the stone on his neck, he was tempted by Satan and sleep fell upon him. Of a sudden he collapsed and fell headlong, and his head was wounded; but he took some of the dust of that place in which he was standing, made the sign of the cross upon it, and closed with it the wound, which immediately was healed so that he had no sort of injury. Afterward he procured a certain round piece of wood, and stood upon it at night, so that if he chanced to fall asleep, the piece of wood would roll from under him.

When the brethren saw his severe toil, and desired to conduct themselves in like manner but were not able, they planned how they might bring false accusation against him. So they said to a certain simple-minded brother of the convent, "Take a dish and put into it morsels of bread and bits of cooked food; then go and show it to the abbot and say to him, 'This food I took from Simeon as he was partaking of it. This mode of life which he keeps up is mere dissimulation.'"

When the abbot heard, he called him and accused him. But he upon this affair returned no answer, because he thirsted that there might be accomplished in him that which our Lord said, "Blessed are ye when men say against you all manner of evil for my sake, falsely."[6] And again the abbot called him and said to him, "Declare if in truth this was spoken about thee," and threatened him with excommunication. Thereupon he revealed to him that it was said about him falsely.

Again, there was there a certain place where wood was piled, and he went and hid himself in it. The brethren thought that he had surely left the convent; but as one of the hebdomadaries went to bring wood he found him standing huddled up in a corner, and came and made it known to the abbot. Then he and the brethren went and entreated him, but he was with difficulty persuaded to go with them and receive the Eucharist.

And again, there went one of the hebdomadaries and heated a poker red-hot and said to him, "If thou hast in thee faith and trustest in thy God, take this poker." He immediately signed himself with the cross and took it with both hands. They expected that nothing would be left of his hands, but he despised them (i.e., his hands), and there was no injury at all done him, for it was as though his hands had been put in cold water. Although great indignation fell upon him from the brethren, yet he did not slacken his toil. After these things he took a hard rope, and wound it round his body many times, until his body swelled out over the rope and hid it. And when the abbot knew it, he compelled him, but with difficulty, to loosen it from him, filled with flesh and blood from his body.

One time as he stood and prayed, Satan appeared to him in the likeness of mist and smote him suddenly upon his eyes and took his vision. And after a long time the abbot besought him to let him bring a physician to see him. But he was unwilling, and said to his brother, "Take me and lead me to the sepulchre in which the blessed ones are placed. I will beseech them, and they will pray for me." And when he had been there three days without sight, in the middle of the night flashes of light appeared to him, until all the house became light from it. And in that hour his eyes were lightened as formerly, and he went to the brethren. And when they saw him, they marvelled at him.

Now there was near the convent a certain cave which was dark and terrible, so that even if in the daytime one saw it he was terrified and trembled, from the sound of roaring which was heard from its interior. And when the fast of the forty days came, this Blessed One went to that cave, and there had many a conflict with Satan. For there came against him serpents and vipers, puffing up and hissing. Moreover, he showed himself in the likeness of a leopard and of terrible beasts. Yet he did not feel afraid at the sight of them, and was not alarmed by their noise, but gave himself over to prayer, and was looking to heaven and making the sign of the cross upon his breast, when suddenly Satan disappeared, vanishing like smoke before the wind. Then a great light shone in that cave, and a voice was heard by the Saint which said, "Lo, the brethren are jealous of thee, and Satan harasses thee; but be strong and of good courage, because the Lord will not let go of thy hands. For lo, his grace keeps thee and his right hand upholds thee, and a head to thy brethren he will make thee, and Satan shall be trampled under thy feet."

When the fast was ended, the brethren sought him in every place and did not find him. And when the abbot saw that he was not there, he said to them, "Take a lamp and go, enter and seek the Blessed One in that cave for our Lord's sake; perhaps he has entered there; let him not die there, lest we be punished for sinning against him." So brethren in whom was the love of our Lord, arose, and took lamps and candles, and entered and sought him diligently, and they found him standing in a certain corner of the cave. Then they led him away and brought him to the convent, and he received the Eucharist with all the brethren.

The brethren then assembled and said to the abbot, "Choose one of two things. Either keep this brother and we will depart, or send him away, and keep us."

But the abbot, because he was not willing to drive away the brethren of his convent, who were a hundred and twenty, pacified them by saying, "If he is not persuaded to put himself on an equality with you, I will do your pleasure."

CHAPTER VI

MAR SIMEON LEAVES THE MONASTERY OF MAR EUSEBONA

And when for a whole year he besought him, and he did not relax from his asceticism, and the brethren did not desist from their importunities, and the fast of the forty days drew near, the abbot summoned him kindly and said to him, "Thou knowest, my son, how much I love thee, and in nothing have I distressed thee, and I have not sought that from here thou shouldst go; but because of the brethren's importunity, and the laws enacted by former abbots, and since I am not able to deviate from their laws, arise, get thee to such a place as our Lord appoints for thee. And if the Lord knows that in heart and truth thou art seeking Him, He, the Lord Himself, will give thee thy petition and thou shalt be head to thy brethren. And this convent in which thou hast been a disciple shall be to thee sustaining and supporting; and I shall hear that the Lord magnifieth thee, and I shall rejoice over thee." Which also happened to him. In the lifetime of his master he became very famous, and his renown went out into the world and before kings, and he heard and rejoiced. And when the abbot finished his course, into the hands of the Blessed One he committed the monastery. He also was a perfect man, who from boyhood to old age had lived in the monastic rule. When he was five years old he entered the convent, and he departed from the world seventy-nine years old, having lived in amazing and wonderful practices. He then gave to the Blessed Mar Simeon four dinars as he arose and departed, and said to him, "These shall be for thy clothing and sustenance until mankind appreciates thee."

And the Holy One on his part said to him, "Far be it from Simeon thy servant that he should hold a dinar in his hand. But instead of these which enrich me not, supply me with prayers which aid me." So he prayed for him and blessed him, saying to him, " Go in peace, and may the Lord be with thee forever."

CHAPTER VII

MAR SIMEON IS LED BY GOD TO THE TOWN OF TELNESHĒ WHERE HE ENDURES THE FAST OF FORTY DAYS

With that separation, therefore, he went out from the convent. And when he had gone a short distance from the convent, he found a road which led to the north. As though it was from the Lord, he turned aside and went in it until he entered the borders of Telneshē. Then he turned aside from the way and stood in prayer under a tree until evening. And he asked in prayer and thus he said: "Oh Lord God, who createdst me in the womb of my mother as thou didst will, and broughtest me forth to this light in thy grace, and implantedst in my mind thy fear as thou didst will, and didst separate me from the house of my fathers in thy mercy, and I have borne thy cross and followed thee according to thy word, and thou hast guarded me from evil and from all their powers in the day of my adversity,—be to me a good guide and protector, that to that place to which thy Glory is pleased, I may come."

And when he finished his prayer, he arose and went down in the way until he came to a certain mountain which was in the town of Telneshē, before the beginning of the fast of the forty days, in the year four hundred and fifty-eight in the chronology of the city of Antioch.[7] There he sat down in a certain valley, considering again in his mind that he would turn to the desert. Then he stood in prayer a long time, and thus he said in his prayer: "O Holy Lord God, if it is thy pleasure that in this town I keep the forty days' fast, at whatever convent I shall knock first let him who comes out answer me and say to me, 'Enter thou, sir,' simply, without investigation."

And when he had finished his prayer, our Lord directed him straight to the convent of Maris bar Barathon of Telneshē, who was the chief of the town. In that time there happened to be there in that convent an old man, a son of the world (i.e., a layman), and a small boy about seven years old. When the holy master knocked, that boy at once went out with great alacrity and opened the door; and when he saw the Blessed One, he greeted him and said to him, "Enter, my master."

The Blessed One said to him, "Go in, my son, make known to the abbot."

The boy said to him, "No, indeed, sir, but do thou enter; I will not let thee go." And he clung to him, and forced him to enter. When he went and told the old man, he also came out quickly and in gladness received him, with affection and love, as though he had known him a long time, since his way was directed from the Lord. And there were no brethren dwelling there, except the old man, and the boy, because it was from the Lord, and they happened to be there and receive him. So he lodged with them in honor.

Then in the morning the Saint said to the old man, "I was seeking a place where I might hide myself in this fast."

He said to him, "Lo, all the convent is before thee. Wherever thou wishest I will make for thee a place." And he sent and called his son, whose name was Maris, and he fixed

17

for him a certain small upper room, which was satisfactory to his mind.

There happened to come there Mar Bas the periodeutes[8] of blessed memory. And he was a man set for a sign, a servant of the Messiah, rejoicing in virtue and far from envy. He was of the people of Edessa of Mesopotamia, a son of senators. And when he had come and talked with the Blessed Mar Simeon, in the love of our Lord, those things which are seemly and becoming to the fear of God, for he was a wise and holy man, then he blessed him and closed the door upon him, and locked it. And he constrained the holy master, and placed with him seven small loaves, and filled a cab[9] of water. And after forty days had passed, the Holy Mar Bas came with great eagerness, and opened the door, and found those seven loaves untouched, and the cab of water full, and the Blessed One kneeling and praying. And every one was astonished and marvelled who happened there, all the more so because at once when they gave him the holy Eucharist[10] he was strengthened and arose and went out with him to the court.

The next day, he sought that he might go to the desert, but they persuaded him, and built for him a cell on the mountain. And there was also in Telneshē a priest at that time, whose name was Daniel, a Christian man. This same one gave a place in his field, where the cell was built.

And the next year, again at the beginning of the fast of the forty days this same master, the Blessed Bas, came and sealed up the door of the cell. And when the forty days were fulfilled, he brought with him the presbyters in whose district he was, and also, with design, some of the periodeutes his companions. And they came and opened the door, and when they gave him the Eucharist, our Lord did there a great miracle. For a certain man from Telneshē who was one of the rulers of the city, whose name was Marenes, brought with him a *hin* filled with ointment. And as Mar Bas stood, and those who came with him, and all the populace, he brought it to the saint that he might bless it. And when he said, "May our Lord bless," at that moment it bubbled up and overflowed like a seething caldron, until all that place was filled with the ointment, and it was poured forth so that all the people took from it. Also they brought many vessels and took from it, yet it was not brought to an end, but filled and overflowing it went down with that man and was in his house, filled, for many years. And healing and remedy in abundance came to everybody from that ointment. This was the first sign which was wrought through the hands of the Blessed Mar Simeon in public, after he had gone out from the convent.

CHAPTER VIII

MAR SIMEON'S BATTLES WITH SATAN

For secretly, also, many battles he had with the Enemy of the good. For Satan brought against him, as he stood and prayed, a black serpent which was very fierce, and it puffed and hissed and threatened him and coiled itself up between his feet, and wound itself about the leg of the holy man many times, up to his knee, and tightened like a rope, as though it would terrify him and take him from prayer. But the Saint was not terrified, but persevered in prayer. And when he had finished his prayer, he raised himself erect, and went out that he might go away. And when he was a little way from it, the messenger of the Lord smote it, and rent it from end to end.

Again, after ten days, as he was standing praying by night, he saw the appearance of a dragon. It was fierce, large and fearful, and changed its appearance. It hissed, and whistled violently, and lashed its tail upon the ground, and rattled and made a noise, so that the earth was moved at the sound it made, and there went out from it as it were flames of fire. Out of its nostrils went forth smoke, and its eyes flashed like lightning. Its length too was considerable. But he, the heroic one, was not daunted, but lifted up his eyes and his hands towards his Lord, and turning blew at it as he said, "Our Lord Jesus Christ rebuke thee." And immediately it vanished, and was not.

CHAPTER IX

THE SICK ARE HEALED AND THE POSSESSED RELEASED THROUGH THE PRAYERS OF MAR SIMEON

The holy Mar Bas, the periodeutes, after he went down from the presence of the blessed master, in the church before all the people, said as with prophetic inspiration, while he marvelled, that many signs our Lord would do by the hands of this Blessed One, so that neither by the hand of a prophet nor by the hand of an apostle had our Lord done more than these. For the kings of the earth and the great ones would come to greet him and prostrate themselves to him, and would seek from him that he should pray for them—which indeed did happen.

Now there was a certain man in the village Yathlaha, which was distant from Telneshē about three miles, who was a rich man and chief of the village, This same man had a daughter who had been a paralytic from the time she was a child, and she had not even been able to move for about eighteen years. They brought her and placed her on the north of the cell, and her father entered and told the Blessed One and besought him to pray for her. And he said to him, "In the name of our Lord Jesus Christ, take some of this dust, and go out, and apply it to her." Now there was no ointment there that might be given, nor could they give any *ḥnāna*,[11] for he had been there only a year and two months. But as soon as that dust touched her in the name of our Lord Jesus Christ, she sprang up, and stood up well; and they gave praise to God, all who saw her. Then on foot she ascended the entire length of the mountain. And her father built for her a convent, and she dwelt in it all the days of her life. This one, then, was the first paralytic who was healed there, and this sign was wrought there, and her father remained with the Blessed One all the days of his life.

After this there came to him two boys who were paralytics, sons of two sisters from the vale of Antioch. One was born paralytic, and the Evil One smote the other six months after he was born and paralyzed him. And a man from Telneshē happened to be passing and saw them, and he told their people about the Blessed One. For hitherto his fame had not gone out. And when they came with them, they brought them in and laid them down before him. As he looked at them he was much moved, because the boys were beautiful. Now they had been in that pitiable condition seven years. And when he finished his prayers, he called those who had brought them and said to them, "Anoint them with this dust in the name of our Lord Jesus Christ." And just as soon as they anointed them, they leaped up and stood and went back and forth before the Blessed One. So they both of them went away healed, rejoicing and praising our Lord.

Again, there came there a certain soldier, who had done a dreadful deed. For as he was going along the road he saw a certain virgin maiden whom he took by force and outraged. And immediately an evil spirit smote him and threw him from his horse, and he withered up like dry wood. He could not talk, neither moved, nor knew any one. And they brought him and laid him before the saint a whole day. When he had ended his prayer, he commanded, and they smeared him with some dust which was before him and also threw water upon him. Then his reason returned, and he sat up, speaking. Then the saint said to him, "Dost thou promise that never again thou wilt do according to that wicked deed?" And he promised that never would he do anything wicked and impious. Thereupon he said to him, "Rise, in the name of our Lord Jesus Christ." And immediately he sprang up and stood and walked. And he went away whole, rejoicing and praising God.

After him there came there a certain man tortured by an evil spirit. For it would lie with him on the bed in the likeness of a woman, and he was greatly tortured and afflicted. When the saint saw him, he said to him, "Anoint thee with that dust in the name of our Lord Jesus Christ, and make with it the sign of the cross three times in thy house, and thou shalt not see it again." And he did as he said to him, and never again an impious thing did he see, until the day of his death.

And in those same days, again, there came to him a certain man from Ḥalab, who brought his son with him bound with chains, because an evil spirit had suddenly come upon him. He would stone his parents with stones, his reason was completely taken away, he wore no clothing at all, and was continually chewing his tongue and biting his arms. And when his father came, he entered and threw himself down before the Blessed One (because up to this time he stood on the ground), and with tears and bitter groans he besought him. And the Blessed One answered and said to the father, "Weep not, but loose from him those bonds." And when his father loosed him, the saint called the boy, and immediately he answered him with joy. And he said to him, "In the name of the Lord Jesus Christ, take some of this dust which is before thee, and anoint all thy body." And the boy himself took it in his hands and anointed all his body. Then he commanded and they brought water, and he blessed it and took it and caused him to drink and threw some on his face. At once his reason returned, and he knew his father, and ran and went and kissed the garments of the saint, and was blessed by him. He lodged there that day, and in the morning went away with his father, healed and praising and blessing God, because He had become his healer through the hands of the saint.

After these things, there was a certain deacon about three miles from the cell, who went out to the harvest, having with him a small boy. As the deacon was reaping and the boy was playing, there went out a fierce black serpent, and coiled himself about the legs of the boy, and began squeezing, while the boy began to howl, calling for help. The deacon, then, when he saw it, said to it, "By the prayers of Mar Simeon who stands in Telneshē, hurt him not." At once it departed from him, and coiled itself up, and was like a string, and did him no hurt at all.

Three days it was thus. And all the village went to see it, and they came and told the Blessed One. He said to that deacon, "Go and say to it, 'In the name of our Lord Jesus Christ, go away and do not hurt any one.'" After that the serpent was released and went away.

Another time they brought to him a boy from the vale, who had a stone in the bladder and was greatly tortured and afflicted. Much money, too, had been spent upon him for physicians, and no one had helped him at all. And when he came to the saint, and he saw him, he gave commandment, and they brought water, and he said to his father, "Put some of that dust in it in the name of our Lord Jesus Christ, and give to him to drink." And immediately when he drank of that water, our Lord gave him deliverance. For there went out from his bladder a round stone, and immediately his internal organs were completely relieved. So he went away well, rejoicing and praising God.

Now an elder of Telneshē loved Mar Simeon greatly, and was with him constantly. The saint's cell stood in his field, and whatever he wore as clothing this elder bought for him at his own expense. And one time the elder came up with all his deacons to the Blessed One, to pay him a visit. And one of those deacons who was steward in the church, joking with him, said to the saint, "Untie that little purse of thine and make a distribution to my master's household."

But he said to him, "Did some one tell thee that I have money, or didst thou perceive it?" And at once his reason turned upside down, and he became as weak as water, and he tore his garments. They took him down, carrying him, and he remained two days in dreadful agonies, tortured, beating his head and gnashing his teeth; then he died.

CHAPTER X

MAR SIMEON ENDEAVORS TO SPEND ONE AND A HALF YEARS IN SECLUSION

After these things the saint formed the purpose of shutting himself up three years, so that he should not see any one and also no one should see him. And he made for himself a chain twenty cubits long, and put it on his leg and fastened it in a rock. It happened that there came along the holy man, the lover of God, Mar Bas, and the elder of the village, and they constrained him by entreaties until he divided those three years in half. Then this Mar Bas constrained him, and left with him a peck and a half of dry pulse, a peck for a year. For he had there a large urn of water, which contained three cabs.

And when he had stopped up the door and was all alone, there suddenly appeared to him the Adversary, who made a great contest with the Blessed One and began to war with him openly. For he came upon him in the likeness of soldiers who were riding horses. And they drew their swords and filled their bows and left their horses for an onrush upon the Blessed One. But he, the holy saint, from the service of his Lord did not cease. Once again they ascended and stood on the wall of the cell and rolled stones down on him, in order that he might betake himself from that place in which he was standing. And one day Satan appeared to him in the likeness of a camel which was lustful and foaming and mischievous, coming and putting its head upon his back. When he reached the Blessed One, there was one in the likeness of an old man standing before the Saint, and he took dust and threw it in the mouth of the camel, when at once it vanished and was not, disappearing like smoke before the wind. Then the old man said to him, "Fear not, be of good courage and be strong."

Another time Satan came with his host, and they were bearing lighted torches. They appeared like flashes of fire ascending even to heaven. Again, they came and stood by him, and were crying and clamoring a long time that they might hinder the Blessed One in his religious exercise. But he was not afraid of them, neither was he terrified by their shriekings, but kept occupied in the service of his Lord. Sometimes they appeared as though destroying rocks and stones, and like the noise of thunder and like the sound of weeping, and as though men, again, were quarrelling with their fellows with spears and swords, and there were some who cried with doleful shrieks, "Thou hast killed me!"

Again Satan appeared to him in the likeness of a lion, which came from the door and opened its mouth, and there went forth from its mouth as it were flames of fire, and it threatened and roared and lifted up its voice, and pawed with its feet and sent the gravel flying clear to the heavens.

Then it rushed upon him violently. While its insane fury continued, after its manner, the Saint did not neglect his religious exercises. Then, again, it vanished like its fellows, and was not.

That abominable one, the doer of evil deeds and lover of wickedness, appeared to the Holy One at midday as he stood praying, in the likeness of a beautiful woman who was clothed with garments of gold and adorned with beautiful things, and she merrily laughed and came towards him. When the Saint saw her, he crossed himself, and turning breathed on her in the name of our Lord Jesus Christ, and immediately she became like a beast whose hands and feet were cut off, and wallowing in howling retreat as though many were pursuing her, until she reached a corner of the cell, she vanished like smoke.

After the saint had been imprisoned five months, and the enemy had warred with him in all forms and appeared to him in all varieties of shape, yet the Blessed One indeed from the service of his Lord had not ceased and from his heavenly labor had not turned, Satan went and collected snakes and scorpions and mice and field-mice and all abominable reptiles, and brought them and filled with them that tank of water which he had there, until it was putrid and the odor went outside of the cell. When the Blessed One saw that the place stank, and he was annoyed by the odor of the stench, he brought earth and stones and filled it.

Many days passed, and when the heat was strong in the month of Tammuz,[12] there was not a drop of water for his drink, and the day on which the door should be opened was still distant thirteen months. Being exceedingly thirsty, he digged in the ground where he was standing, and kneeled and put his mouth in it, breathing the coolness of the clay. Then he stretched his hands towards heaven and prayed, and thus he said in his prayer, "O Mighty Lord, possessor of heaven and earth, according as thy Divinity knoweth deal with thy servant." And he continued in prayer to God a long time. When he arose from his prayer and crossed himself, he turned to his right hand and saw a brook filled with water, clear and cool and sweet. And when he saw it, he thought it was an illusion. And he came and prayed by it no little time. But the waters did not remove from their place, so he knew that this thing was from God to him; and it remained for his use until the day the cell was opened.

His clothing was patched with straw from the wild grain of the second year, which grew before him in the enclosure, and upon it he coiled a hard rope. With this clothing he was clothed seven years; then he made him a cloak of goat leather.

Thus evil was put to confusion with all its retinue, and the Messiah was glorified by his faithful servant.

May our Lord be adored for his loving kindness! He did not leave his athlete in this contest, but speedily sent him consolation and comfort. For there appeared to him, after that commotion and clamor and strife, a beautiful man who was covered with a white stole, who came and stood in front of the window of the sacred treasury and folded his hands behind him. And he bowed and raised himself up many times. And when he had finished his prayer, he went to the eastern wall, and spreading out his hands to heaven, prayed a considerable time, then disappeared. From him, therefore, the Blessed One learned this custom, by which he bowed and stood up. For he knew and understood that that was the care of our Lord.

Now again after this there appeared to him beautiful boys who were clothed in white and bearing wax-candles lighted and golden crosses. They stood by the wall and just before the window of the sacred treasury, and sang praises, saying, "Blessed is the Lord who chose the elect in a strong city." And many times was heard there the voice of worship and of praise and of adoration, so that many of the people of the village, they who were passing the night in the threshing-floors and were rising early to go to work, heard the sound, and also saw the vision.

For no one began to lodge in the mandra, until Satan incited the robbers and brought against him three of them. They came and descended from the wall at midnight, and one of them drew his sword and rushed violently against him. The other two raised their spears against him, which were bound with iron. But as that first one ran violently on and came, suddenly our Lord smote him upon his face and dimmed his eyes, and he swayed like a reed. And he was paralyzed and dropped down, his sword falling from his hands. Then, his mouth closed, he stood up there in that place, unable to move to either side. His companions, too, likewise continued, speechless, upon their spears, with their mouths closed. And at dawn they were standing, and so stood all day in extreme misery, bowed before him.

When it was evening the Blessed One spoke with them and said to them, "Whence come ye? And what seek ye?"

Thereupon two of them in great agony said to him, "We came as robbers, and descended that we might kill thee." One, indeed, could not open his mouth, but with closed mouth thus he remained.

Thereupon the Holy One cried out (for them) three times, and at once they could uproot their legs from the ground. Then he said to them, "Go away, and do not again harm any one, lest ye suffer worse than this."

Now after those days of his imprisonment, when the year and a half was fulfilled, the Holy Mar Bas came, and a considerable crowd collected. And they opened the door and gave him the Eucharist. That very day our Lord exhibited loving kindness and shewed a marvellous sign.

28

They opened the mortar into which had been put the lentils which the Holy Mar Bas left for him, and they found it full, just as they had left it, and they wondered and were astonished. Then the elders and deacons arose, and gave a present from it to all the people, from three o'clock even until nine, and it was not exhausted. Then there went up also widows of the city, and received their skirts full and went down, and still it remained just as it was. And also at this Mar Bas greatly wondered. Every one else wondered at it, too, for this was a marvellous thing.

CHAPTER XI

MAR SIMEON SETS UP HIS FIRST COLUMN; THE DECEASE OF HIS BROTHER MAR SHEMSHI

After these things he set up a stone, that he might stand upon it, that had four bases and was two cubits high.

Mar Bas, however, excused himself from further visiting and entered and dwelt in his convent, and our Lord gave prosperity in his hands, and he built an excellent monastery in which our Lord took pleasure.

After these things the Saint's fame began to be talked about in the world, and men began to flock to him from everywhere. For he stood upon that stone five years. And his fame began to spread abroad to all quarters, and men resorted to him from every place. And after the five years which he stood upon the stone, his brother Mar Shemshi fell asleep in good renown and works of righteousness. This thing also our Lord revealed to him, and did not hide from him concerning his departure. For, three days before, he called three elders, chiefs of the city, Marenes and Demetrianus and Maris, and said to them, "Before the door of this cell is opened, Mar Shemshi my brother will depart this life. But make a shrine and put him in it, and take heed that no one take him from you."

For he saw thus: a certain tree which was loaded with much fruit and beautiful in its appearance, with its top branches adorned and leafy and full of fruit, and its leaves pleasant to see, and to behold they were very delightful. And there was a certain branch in it which was shooting out from it. And there came a certain man of good appearance, whose aspect was very wonderful, and led with him four men who carried axes in their hands, and he said to them, "Cut down this branch from this tree, for it greatly hinders it, and keeps it from bearing much fruit."

And lo, still another man appeared, who stood by it, who also on his part was adorned in his apparel and comely in his visage, and this man said, "Let us make another companion for it."

But he answered and said to him, "A companion is not needed for it, for it is sufficient by itself both for those outside and for those inside"

And when the branch was taken from the tree, the man commanded those four men and said to them, "Dig now, and go deep, and let the root of this tree be placed upon the rock, and fill up, going up even to its topmost branches, and let it be made very firm that it may not be shaken. For much is the fruit it will bear, and strong winds and billows and violent tempests will strike it."

And as they digged deep and placed it, firmly setting its root, it put forth new shoots, and branching threw out limbs to all quarters, and bore much fruit, a hundredfold over that it had formerly borne. And beneath the root of that tree there sprang up suddenly a fountain of mighty waters, and covered the mountains and hills, and it shot up and sprang up to the four quarters. And lo, again, suddenly there appeared much animal life, and birds innumerable, of every species and every form, great and small, from all quarters resorting and coming, eating of the fruit of that tree and drinking from the fountain. And in proportion as they ate and drank from it, the fruit of the tree increased and abounded, and the fountain also was mighty and strong gushing. The tree was Mar Simeon, and the branch which was cut from it Mar Shemshi his brother. When the days of his brother were finished, he departed from the world, just as he had said in those days of the retirement in the cell.

CHAPTER XII

MAR SIMEON'S FAME SPREADS ACROSS THE WORLD

When the day came and the door of the mandra of the saint was opened, God stirred up all mankind, as though a heavenly command from on high were upon all the world, and creation was moved that it should come; for there was no limit or reckoning to it, and the mountains were covered and the highways were filled. And no one could see any other thing except that human throng; it was not possible to know who were halting, nor who were setting out. His fame spread to the four quarters of creation, and it increased and became known unto the King of the West. And again, his fame was heard also even by the King of the East.

Our Lord began to do and show by his hand wonderful miracles and marvellous wonders. And the gift of healing was given him from God, the story of which is too great for the mouth of mortal man. And was fulfilled the word of the apostle who said, "The gift of God is greater than we can tell." For what mouth of mortal man can venture to tell it; or what witness be found to record it, or what intelligence so sound as to be able to count or compute it; what benefits were from God by the hand of the Blessed Mar Simeon to all mankind? For how many afar off were brought near!

And how many were wandering astray and by his word were turned from error to a knowledge of truth! How many thousands and tens of thousands who heard his commands were brought home and submitted themselves to the yoke of Christ! For who is he will count or reckon the thousands and the tens of thousands innumerable, who while savage came to the sight of him, and to his word and to his teaching divine, and joyfully surrendered themselves to the fear of Christ, and became workers and servants of the Truth! For the fame of his benefactions spread, which our Lord did by his hand, from end to end of creation. And that was fulfilled which the Prophet said,[13] "Their glad message is gone out in all the earth and their words to the ends of the world."

For letters of kings poured in, and by the hand of messengers in writings, petition and request with captains of their hosts they were sending to his righteousness. And they besought from his holiness that he would bless them and pray for their kingdom, and the rulers who were under their power, and that he would command them all whatever he pleased. For joyfully without refusal they received his word, and in the beginning of their letters, "father and teacher who from God is given to us," they addressed him. And they implored him that freely he would command concerning everything. But whatever praised and glorified God and was for their soul's welfare and of help to the poor and establishing their kingdom, he counseled and advised them. But those kings, with the princes who were under the authority of their kingdom, joyfully received the answer of the letters of the Blessed One, and quickly did all that he commanded as his pleasure. And they praised God concerning the reports, news, and good things which they heard. And was fulfilled concerning him, the holy saint, that which our Lord said in his Gospel, "Blessed is the servant on account of whom the name of his Lord is praised." For by his diligence and his toil he was the cause of advantage to himself and to many, and the name of God was praised on his account and for his sake, from the rising of the sun unto its going down.

How many thousands and myriads who were even unconscious that there is a God, through the saint came to know God their Creator and became his worshippers and adorers! Again, how many unclean were sanctified, and how many licentious became chaste at sight of him! How many, also, who were not persuaded in the fear of our Lord, who came to hear him from distant places, when they saw his beautiful person and his discipline and never-ending toil, despised and left the transitory world with all that is in it, and became disciples of the word of truth, and many of them were vessels of honor! Again, how many harlots came there and from afar saw him, the Holy One, and renounced and left their places and the cities in which they had lived, and surrendered themselves to the Christ, and entering dwelt in convents and became vessels of honor, and with their tears they served their Lord and blotted out the list of their debts!

How many distant Arabs who did not even know what bread is, but whose subsistence was the flesh of animals, when they came and saw the Blessed One, became disciples and were Christians and renounced the images of their fathers and served God! How many barbarians and Armenians and Aurtians and pagans of every tongue came continually, and every single day crowd upon crowd received baptism and confessed the living God! And there was no end to the Arabs and their kings and chiefs who there received baptism and believed in God and confessed the Messiah, and at the word of the Blessed One also built churches among their tents!

How many oppressed were released by his word from

their oppressors! How many bills of debt were torn up by his effort! How many maltreated were relieved from those who led them in bonds! How many slaves, too, were manumitted, and their documents torn up before the Holy one! How many orphans and widows were sustained and supported (after our Lord) by the standing of the Blessed One! His Lord did these things by his hands. He also magnified the priests of God sedulously, and the regulations and laws of the church were established by his care. He also gave command regarding usury, that one half of the usury on everything should be taken; and every person in joy received his command, so that there were many who remitted the whole of it and did not exact usury after he had commanded.

Now concerning the healing which our Lord gave through his hands, and how much deliverance and benefit came to men through his prayer, and to how many afflicted lives which had been crushed and tortured by smitings of various sorts from the workings of the Devil, by the hands of the Blessed Mar Simeon God was pleased to give alleviation and free them from the servitude of the Fiend, this for the mouth of mortals is too great to speak about. How many thousands and tens of thousands of afflicted, to whom our Lord gave help and deliverance, went away rejoicing from the presence of the Blessed One, praising God. And that was fulfilled concerning the Blessed One, which our Lord said, "Those who believe in me, the works which I do shall they do, and greater than those."

For what mouth would dare to tell or count or reckon the benefits even of one year which were conferred in the mandra of the Blessed One, to say nothing of fifty years! How many lepers were purified there! How many blind were led when they came, but, after our Lord had permitted them to see the light, went away praising God!

How many hunchbacked, too, were straightened out by his prayers! Again, how many paralytics were conveyed there like luggage, and some of them, also, on litters, who were even unable to move, and our Lord by his prayer gave them help and deliverance, and they went out from his presence healed, running and rejoicing and carrying their couches and praising God who had magnified his loving kindness to them! But because your mind is very eager to hear the exploits of holy men, and your attention desirous to learn what was done from God through his servants, and how much, too, he exalted and honored those who loved him, as much as our mind can, we will narrate a few things out of the many. For who is it measures the great abyss or counts the sand which is on the sea-shore, but God who made them? Thus, also, the treasures of the faithful and the exploits of the blessed ones there is no one who knows, except God their Creator.

CHAPTER XIII

MAR SIMEON BEGINS HIS MINISTRY FROM THE PILLAR

The beginning, then, of the monastic life of the saint in the mandra was thus. He stood on a stone in the northwest corner of the mandra. Every year, during the holy days of the Lenten fast, he remained shut up in the mandra without food and drink until the day of the Passover, being tempted by the evil Enemy of mankind, who envies the grace of the good and is the enemy of righteousness. He appeared to him in various forms, in a variety of moulds, like vipers and other serpents, just as he had appeared to him in the cave when he went out from the monastery; and they coiled themselves on his body with many threatenings, breathing fire, in order to turn him away from confidence in his Creator. But he stood in his integrity, and did not remove his eyes from heaven. And in the fast of the forty days Satan appeared to him in the form of a lion, and of a dragon which coiled itself all about his body and stung him on his foot. He had no power over him, it was only that his Creator would show him that he had a human body. And in all this contest and war he was not brought down from his integrity, but Satan continued in his discomfiture and cried out, and howled with the rest of his hosts, and said, "Woe to us! Because the shame which we received from Job is renewed to us in Simeon who is from Ṣīṣ!" Many times this happened, yet he did not turn around, but stood in prayer uninterruptedly.

And every year, every fast of the forty days, food such as is suitable for men did not come to his mouth. And many whom they brought with severe afflictions were healed by his prayers. A certain monk, a paralytic, whose shanks were cleaving to his thighs, came to him, as they carried him, and they laid him down before the Saint. And with eyes lifted toward heaven, and standing in prayer, he besought the Lord in his behalf. Thereupon his legs were suddenly straightened, and he stood up and leaped before him like a hart, shouting with a loud voice, with the rest of the many people who were there, praising and blessing God, who had strengthened his weak limbs.

And after a while many people in the village of Telneshē were struck with sicknesses of severe tumors, so that many of them passed away from earth with the tumor-disease. Then all of them assembled and went up to the Blessed One and entreated him to offer petition on their behalf to God, that they might be delivered from the severe sicknesses which were sent upon them. Now as he stood in prayer, a certain stone eucharistic chalice was placed in the window which was before him. And as all of the assembly of the people stood, and petitioned and prayed him on behalf of their sicknesses, he lifted his eyes to heaven and prayed. And as he offered his prayer, suddenly that cup was filled with water, and overflowed on all sides upon the ground. And all the people ran, and rubbed themselves with the water, and immediately they were cured of the sickness of their tumors.

Again, a certain great man from the order of the nobles, who was an inhabitant of the West, who had heard the fame of the Blessed One, was lying ill of severe sickness, of a flux of blood of years' duration, so that on account of it he also endured severe trials, such that he was unable to put clothes on his body, because of the flux of his blood. This was a secret, however, not revealed to any one, on account of his noble extraction. But he came to the Blessed One and besought him that from the hard trial which was upon him he might be delivered by his prayers. So he prayed for him to God, and the afflicted was delivered from his sickness. And he went to his house, exulting and praising God on account of the healing which had been given him by the prayers of the man of God.

And a certain woman who was led by an evil spirit and was in grievous torment and had not one quiet hour from the plague but was rent by the devil, so that blood flowed from her mouth, she too came to the mandra of the Holy One. And when the many people saw her, they made a request of the Holy One in her behalf that he should petition God for her that she might be cured of her severe affliction. And he prayed to God and besought in her behalf. Then he dispatched a certain man of those who stood before him and sent word to the devil who was speaking by the mouth of that woman, "In the name of our Lord Jesus Christ I command thee to be still and not talk." In that very hour the unclean spirit departed from her, and she was healed of her devil.

Again, a certain great man, governor of a certain city of the land of Palestine, who was a heathen, had his head bent and his neck placed on his breast so that he could not lift his head up. But he came to the man of God, borne by two on a litter. And they presented a request that he would ask mercy from God upon him, while he informed him that many physicians had given him up, and he had spent much money on account of his sickness with sorcerers and magicians, yet was not one whit better of his disease. And he cried out and said before him, as he clasped his feet and supplicated him, "From thee I will not depart, and from the door of thy God I will not remove, and my hands from thy feet I will not lift, and the prayer thou dost offer to God I will not allow thee, until thou dost place thy hands upon my head."

And while he was thus speaking, he did not allow the man of God to pray. But the blessed saint answered him, saying, "I am a sinful man and least of all men, and my hands are not like those of all the rest of the bishops and monks which they placed upon thee. And one thing I say to thee, that for a man to heal a man without the will of God is impossible. But I will commit thee to the hands of the living God, he who made the world in his mercy and his grace, he who can heal thee from the terrible affliction which thou hast."

Thereupon he left off holding the feet of the Saint. Now it was his custom that at the time when he finished his prayer he knocked with his foot upon the little bench[14] which was placed against the rock on which he was standing. So when he reached the time for the ending of prayer, immediately he struck with his foot, and all of those who had been kneeling before him during the prayer started and stood up. And at once the afflicted one stood up healed from his sickness, his head lifted up from his breast, and he praised God with all the rest of the people who were there, because of the benefit

38

and the healing which he had received. Much gold for the sake of his healing he offered to the man of God. But the Blessed One replied to him, saying, "I have no need of gold or silver. But I ask for thee that the light of truth may lighten thee through holy baptism for the forsaking of thy sins, and that thou shouldst free thy slaves who carried thee, that by their freedom thou mayst free thyself from Satan." When he heard the words of the Blessed One, everything that he commanded him he did, then went home in peace and in health, as he praised God, because by the hand of his holy servant he was healed from his affliction.

And after a long time there was a lack of rain in the land of the east and in this land, such that the earth on account of the drought was near to fail to produce seed. And many people assembled from the east with the inhabitants of the mountain, and came with a request to the man of God, beseeching him and supplicating him that he would ask his God concerning this thing, that he should have compassion, and give hope to creation. He answered them, saying, "Turn to God and bring an offering to the Lord your God; turn away from evil and do good; then, turning, immediately he will have mercy upon you." So they did as he commanded them; whereupon the clouds poured forth rain and filled their cisterns as usual. And the reaper filled his hand, and the poor ate and were satisfied, and they praised and blessed God their nourisher.

Then the man of God made a vow between himself and his God, saying, "Because thou hast received my prayer, which in behalf of the poor and needy I brought to thee, I will appoint a memorial day and will present an offering to thee my Lord." Now it happened that on the first memorial day which he celebrated, people were gathered together without number, so that the mountains were covered with them. And there came seven tormented children who had been paralytics from their mothers' wombs, and they laid them down before him. He gazed on them, and lifting his eyes to heaven prayed, and committed them to the hands of God their Creator. And immediately their limbs became strong, and standing up they leaped for joy before him. Then all the people who were assembled together there offered praise to God, who had given power such as this to men.

CHAPTER XIV
VARIOUS MIRACULOUS HEALINGS OF MAR SIMEON

Again, there came to him a certain rich man from Sheba, who had an illness severe and serious. For a grievous disease had besieged him in his brain for many years. He had incurred great expense for physicians; yet no one had helped him at all, but the affliction was all the more severe. Four spikes were fixed for him in the wall, and he sat between them and knocked and buffeted his head against this side and that. And when he learned about the saint from the merchants who went down to that place, he gave up and left all that he possessed, that only he might get help for himself. And he took with him five of his servants and five steeds, and furnished himself with food, and set out to come to the Saint. But God, who saw his faith, wrought a great miracle in his case. For they were people who knew not the way, and the country was difficult desert; but thus they narrated, that, as though some one were leading their camels, so they came on without either losing the way or even becoming confused. And no man from the Arab marauding bands harmed them, neither did wild beasts injure them, although lions abounded in all that region. And the disease, after he set out to come, on each succeeding day grew better. And more than all of these things, so they told us, those provisions which they had laid in did not lack anything but thus remained as they were when they set out with them, although they were living upon them until they rested at the mandra of the saint, for a full year.

And when he entered he cast himself before the Holy One, and made known everything just as it was, and how many pains and afflictions he had borne, lo, these many years. He commanded, and they brought water, and when he had prayed and blessed it, he commanded him in the name of Christ, and he drank of it; then he threw some on his head, and as soon as this water touched him, his disease fled from him, and he never felt it again, and all his body was relieved and quieted. Then he praised and blessed God and, receiving baptism, became a Christian. And finally, also, he departed this world with a great testimony.

Again, there came to him a chorepiscopus from the Persians, whom one of the Persian kings had sent. For he (the king) had an only son whom Satan had smitten so that he was paralyzed, and had been laid upon a bed fifteen years. Unless some one turned him over on his side, he did not move. He had given great wealth to the Magians and to the Sorcerers, but they did not help him at all. When he learned about the saint, he persuaded this same chorepiscopus and sent him, that he might beseech of the holy and pious one that he would pray for his son. He sent by him two silk hangings, very costly, ornamented with golden crosses all over them. And when he came and told the saint about the affliction of the boy, and then also showed those hangings, he said to him, "Take them with thee in the name of our Lord Jesus Christ as they are tied up, and go in peace. And when thou hast arrived at the boundary of the city, descend from thy ass, and take them in thy arms, and give no answer to any one. But enter carefully, and put them upon the breast of the boy and say to him, 'The sinner Simeon saith in the name of our Lord Jesus Christ, "Stand up."' And he went and did just as he commanded him, and the moment he placed them upon his heart and said to him as it had been commanded him, his disease departed from him and he sprang to his feet cured. And he rejoiced, and praised and glorified God. And he became a Christian and received baptism, he and his mother and his sister. And after a little while he came and was blessed by Mar Simeon, confessing the goodness which our Lord had shown to him; then he went away to his land in peace.

Another time there came to the Saint a certain governor from Armenia, son of the ruler of all that land, who was highly esteemed by the king, to whom also the king had sometime given purple garments. He was suddenly attacked with partial paralysis, and his whole right side was withered, and his mouth was twisted, and his eye was fixed; and he had been bedridden for many years with many pains, without being able to turn from one side to the other. And besides, neither did he eat anything, except a spoonful of liquid with great distress. Then when the fame of the saint reached them, they put him in a litter, and took him up that they might bring him. Many people came with him, armed, horsemen, and servants with much baggage. Besides, there also came with him three elders and five deacons, with letters from the bishops of all that country, who had written to Mar Simeon a request that he would pray over him. For they loved him much, because he was a lovable youth, and his father was a believer and one who honored the Christians.

When they had brought him in and placed him before the Reverend Sir, and the letters from the bishops had also been read, he sighed and raised his eyes towards heaven and pronounced a prayer over him with all the people. Having finished the prayer, he commanded and they brought water, which he blessed; then at his word they cast some of it upon him, and he cried and said to him, "In the name of our Lord Jesus Christ, sit up." And at once he turned himself and sat up, and his reason returned, and he knew where he was. The saint said to him, "Take some of this water in the name of the Lord Jesus Christ, and do thou drink some of it with thy own hands, and put some on thy face and upon all thy body." And he took and drank and put some upon all his body. He said to him, "In the name of our Lord Jesus Christ, stand up." And he sprang up cured. Then he ran back and forth in the mandra praising and blessing God, and he, too, a man who had been unable to turn over in his bed. He stayed there one week standing in prayer; and he manumitted three slaves. Then he entered Antioch, and came and prayed and received a blessing, and went away to his land in peace and in tranquility, praising and blessing God and all his worshippers.

Again, there came some Easterners from a land so distant, they were a year and a month in reaching the mandra, as they informed the saint, four men who were full of leprosy, and three who were possessed of evil spirits. And when they entered, they cast themselves before him and told him of their affliction and the remoteness of their home. And they even opened their purses, and showed in the sight of the people, and said, "These are the provisions with which we furnished ourselves at home and set out. Today, lo, it is thirteen months that we have journeyed, and neither have we lost the way nor been in trouble."

And when the Saint heard their words, he said to them, "That God who guarded the way before you, He also will grant that thing for the sake of which you have suffered." Then at his command they brought water, and he blessed it and said to them, "Take this in the name of our Lord Jesus Christ, in the hope of whom ye came, and drink some

of it, all of you, and also cast some all over your body"
They did as he commanded them; when immediately their
diseases vanished, and they were cleansed and recovered
of their illnesses. And they praised and blessed God, and
renouncing their superstitions they received baptism and
became Christians. Then they departed rejoicing and
adoring our Lord.

Again, there came there from inner Anaziṭ, which is on
the border of Armenia and Persia, in the days of Dionysius
the military officer, a youth who had a severe and obstinate
affliction. For suddenly a pain seized him in his head, his
face swelled, and his sight was taken away, while his whole
body became limp and weak, and the mucus which came
from his nose and eyes had an extremely offensive odor.
When his father heard the report about the Blessed One,
he sent his son to Dionysius the military commander, and
wrote asking him to use his influence with the Reverend
Sir for his sake; he also sent heavy gifts by his hand. And
Dionysius himself sent with him Dalmatius his sister's son.
When they arrived and entered, they cast him before the
Blessed One and told him whence he was, and about his
affliction, how severe it was. He commanded, and they
loosened the bandages with which his head and face were
wrapped about. Then he cried out to him and said, "Stand
up, in the name of our Lord Jesus Christ." And immediately
he sprang to his feet. Then he continuing said to him, "Go,
in the name of our Lord Jesus Christ, and take for thyself
in thy hands some of this water, and cast it upon thy face
and all over thy body." And the very moment that the water
touched him in the name of our Lord, his affliction vanished
from him and he was recovered and completely restored.
And he came in and went out, and was with the Saint three
days; then he went home, well and praising God. And when
Dionysius the commander heard of it, he was amazed and

marvelled and was confirmed in the Faith.

Neither in the case of Dionysius himself was the kindness small which was performed in him by God by the hand of the Saint. For when he came to Antioch, he received letters from the Emperor that he should go down with an embassy to the Persians. Then suddenly Satan smote him on his face, so that his mouth was distorted and his whole face drawn to one side. The physicians came and gave him roots and salves, but he was not benefited at all. Then he came to the Saint, in distress, and said to him, "I have received letters from the Emperor that I should go down to the Persians. And lo, suddenly, what has happened to me! But I beseech thee, pray for me."

And he gave command, and they brought water, and he prayed and blessed it and said to him, "In the name of our Lord Jesus Christ, take it in thy hand and throw some on thy face and on thy head." And when he threw it as he commanded him, his face was restored, and his mouth, as though it had never been injured. And he burst out into exultation and blessed and praised God. The Saint said to him, "Go, and may the Lord God prosper thee on this journey, and thou do all which thou seekest, and go down in peace and come again in safety." The Lord prospered his way, and he was received magnificently and accomplished what he sought, and when he went up with pomp and honor, he came and prostrated himself before the Saint and received a blessing from him. And all the days of his life, whatever the Saint commanded him in behalf of the poor or about any matter, he gladly accepted, did obeisance, and performed his command.

CHAPTER XV

THE POWER OF MAR SIMEON'S PRAYERS OVER NATURAL PHENOMENA AND WILD ANIMALS

Another time there came to him a certain elder from the region of Samosata, about seven days' journey. He told him about the fountain of his town, which watered all the fields of their town, and from which, after our Lord, was their supply for living. It suddenly failed and went dry, and they were troubled with thirst and for food. And they had sought workmen, who had digged and delved, and expended much money upon it, but they could not find a drop of water in it. And when the elder came and told him this thing, the Saint said to him, "I have confidence in the Lord Jesus, that even while you are going out of this mandra our Lord will permit it to come to its normal condition. But go keep vigil and celebrate mass and make it known to our Lord." Then that presbyter noted down the time in which the Blessed One said it to him. And he went and found that the fountain had begun to flow and was gushing out and watering all those fields twofold more than it ever had. Then he took out the memorandum which he had made, and it was found that at the very time the saint was blessing the elder the fountain had burst forth in its usual condition. The elder then led out all his constituency, and they came and held divine service before the saint three days; then went back praising and blessing God.

Again, another elder from the region of Dalok: a certain mountain was near their village, about two miles off, and it kept creeping nearer little by little until it touched the border of the village. And from under it was heard the sound of waters, mighty as the abyss, and from their fear all the inhabitants of the village had forsaken it and fled. It was fearful, because they saw the mountain creeping and coming to bury them. And when they saw that calamity was fated for them, and there was no help anywhere, the presbyter arose and brought his whole village, from the greatest even to the smallest and came to the blessed Mar Simeon. When they entered, they all cast themselves down before him and told him the whole matter. He said to them, "In the name of our Lord Jesus Christ, take three stones, and make three crosses upon them, and go fix them before it, and there keep vigil three days and celebrate the mass. And I have confidence in the Lord that it will not come any nearer." And our Lord did there a great sign. For they went and did as he had commanded them, and on the third day of a sudden was heard from beneath the mountain the sound of a mighty crash like thunder, and the mountain sank away. And there went up from beneath it many waters and covered all that land. Then our Lord dried them up, and after three days the water was all swallowed up, and no damage was done. The mountain had become level with the earth, and was like a plain. They sowed it that year with vetches, and got from it two hundred cors.[15] They carried loads of them on camels and beasts of burden, and divided among the monks and poor, while they confessed before everyone the kindness which had been wrought for them.

Again: another elder from the region of Marᶜash, whom some business called to go to another village. As he went on the way in the mountain with two brothers of his, and rode on an ass, lo, eleven goats, such as are called mountain-goats, came to pass before him. And from a distance he cried out, to make a test, saying to them: "By the prayer of Mar Simeon, be ye bound, that ye may not pass until I come to you." And they all collected and stood quiet until he came to them. And he dismounted from the ass and caught two or three of them, and put his hand upon their backs and stroked them, and they stood still. And he was astonished and marvelled. Then after a little while he said to them: "By the prayer of the holy Mar Simeon, cross over and go your way;" and thereupon they left him. Then he from fear and distress on account of what he had done felt something seize his heart and choke him. And he did not even enter his village but went back to the Saint, with a color like death, and entering fell down before him, and told all these things publicly, how the thing happened, with tears.

Then when the Saint heard it, he said, "Lo, the beasts obey the word of God, but men resist his will." To the elder he said, "Take some of this water and throw it upon thy face and upon thy breast, in the name of Christ, and go fast three days and celebrate mass to God; and do not tempt the spirit of God, lest wrath come upon thee." Then he went away restored from his affliction.

Again, one time a fierce lion was seen on Mt. Ukkama ("Black Mountain") where a lion had never been seen before, and it devoured many people and made bitter havoc among men. For it ate and wounded many people without number, and travel was hindered. For no one dared to go outside the door of his house, nor go out to work, nor go on a journey, from fear. For in one day it was seen in many places. And the report of it spread into the cities, and the prefects also heard it. And they sent out many hunters, while the soldiers and Isaurians furnished spears and swords, but no one did him any harm. For he made light of many, and at his roaring a multitude of people trembled in fright. Now when a long time had elapsed, and he did not cease to slaughter many, numerous people assembled from the north and came and told the Saint, saying to him, "He enters among flocks and herds, but leaves the cattle and eats men."

And when the holy master learned about his depredations and how many people he had destroyed, he said, "I have confidence in the Lord Jesus Christ that he will never harm the shape of man again. But take in the name of Christ some of this *ḥnāna* and this ointment, and wherever you see him, whether crouching or standing, make the sign of the cross on all sides of him. And lo, the Angel of the Lord will paralyze him."

And our Lord showed his mercy manifestly. For while those men who had told him were going on their journey, he happened to be crouching before them. When he saw them, he sprang up as was his wont; part trembled as they saw him and were affrighted. But as he made ready to spring upon them, he swayed and tottered and sank down. Then again he arose, and again fell. Thereupon they perceived that he was smitten of the Lord, and one of them took a spear and approaching struck him in his heart and killed him. Then they skinned him, and came to the mandra of the blessed master, who for this thing also greatly praised and blessed our Lord. For the depredation had been severe and grievous.

CHAPTER XVI

A PARALYTIC PRESBYTER IS HEALED THROUGH THE INTERCESSION OF MAR SIMEON

Again after these things they brought to the Saint a certain elder from the north, who was prostrated with a severe and bitter affliction. For while he was sitting reading the scripture in the court of the church, on a sudden he saw that something was passing before him in the likeness of a mist; and the Evil One, the enemy of mankind, smote him upon his face, and threw him down upon the ground. And his sight left him, his reason fled, he became rigid like wood, all his limbs became impotent, and he could not speak. And they came in and found him stretched out like one dead.

They picked him up and put him on a bed, and he was in that affliction nine years, while he uttered not a word, nor knew any one. Neither could he turn over, unless some one turned him.

When they heard about the Saint, they took him up to bring him on the couch to Mar Simeon. And when they arrived at Shīḥ, a village which was distant from Telneshē three miles, they spent the night there, they who were carrying him, because of the great toil and from the weariness of the way, that they might rise early and go up to the Saint. But God who saw the faith and work of those who brought him, and the affliction and trouble of the elder, which had lasted all this long time, did not withhold from him the gift of mercy but performed loving kindness with him openly. For as the Saint was standing praying, it was revealed to him by the spirit of God about the distress of the afflicted presbyter, and in what manner and by whose agency the disease had come upon him. So at midnight he summoned one of his attendants and said to him, "Take a little water in a vessel, and arise, go down to Shīḥ. And in the court of the church thou wilt find a certain elder who is a paralytic, wasted, and bedridden. Throw some of this water on him and say to him: 'The sinner Simeon says, In the name of our Lord Jesus Christ leave thy couch in the church, and arise, walk, and come on thy feet. Long enough others have carried thee, henceforth the grace of thy Lord will strengthen thee.'"

Then the attendant went down and found in the church, as he had said to him, that he was lying on his couch as though dead, in that great anguish. And as they saw the attendant, many people gathered about him, and in their presence he threw the water upon him, and as Mar Simeon had commanded him he said to him, "Mar Simeon the Blessed said, 'Arise in the name of Christ, and walk thou on thy feet and come to me.'" And as soon as the water touched him, with the blessing by the mouth of the servant of God Mar Simeon, his diseases fled from him, he was recovered of his distress, and he came to his senses and saw the light,[16] and recovered his strength, and all his members grew strong and vigorous. He leapt to his feet from his couch, entirely well, and entering prayed in the church, praising and blessing God, who had shown such grace manifestly through the Saint. Then he went up afoot, accompanied by many people who blessed and praised God for the manifest miracle which their eyes had seen. For they saw him who had been bedridden, like an empty vessel which is useless, that as soon as the water touched him with the blessing of the mouth of the Holy One, he sprang up from his couch as though no injury or disease had ever touched him in his life.

And when he went up and entered the mandra and prostrated himself before the Blessed One, he said to him, "Arise and fear not. For even if Satan hath sought to distress thee through his agents and the servants of his will, yet the mercies of God have been manifested upon thee, and he hath shown thee loving kindness. And as for those through whom came upon thee the trouble, lo, thou art about to find them in affliction and distress, and they will beseech of thee and implore thee to forgive them. As God hath had mercy upon thee, so also do thou forgive the folly of those who wronged thee. Take a little *ḥnāna* and water, and anoint them, and God will have mercy upon them." Then the elder went, meanwhile rejoicing and praising and blessing our Lord, he and his companions, and found those his enemies in anguish and great trouble, as the Saint had said to him. But when he threw the water on them and anointed them with the *ḥnāna*, our Lord willed it, and they recovered. Then they arose and came to the Saint's mandra, and before

51

him in a public manner each one confessed his folly. He commanded and warned them, and they too went away recovered, rejoicing and praising God.

CHAPTER XVII

MAR SIMEON AIDS THE POOR
AND BRINGS JUSTICE UPON THE WICKED

Again, there came to him a certain poor man from the region of Ḥalab, weeping in distress and grief of heart. When he entered, he prostrated himself before the Saint and said to him, "Master, I seek thine aid. I hired a field and made a cucumber garden in it, that I might provide from it for myself and the orphans whom I have. But when it began to grow, some men came by night and rooted up the entire field, leaving nothing in it except ten beans." And he brought some of them and threw them down before him.

Thereupon the Saint said to him, "Arise and do not be grieved; for the savor of death strikes me from this affair. But take some of this *ḥnāna* and go make three signs of the cross in the name of our Lord Jesus Christ in that field. And I have confidence in our Lord, that if there remains but three sprouts for thee there, the Lord will bless them, and three times as much as you expected will be produced from them. As for those who did you this damage, quickly the judgment of God will overtake them. Because they dared to treat with contempt the longsuffering of God, therefore quickly his justice will lay them low. For there are three of them, and they have committed great injuries upon churches and monasteries, and caused grief to many. Now punishment is coming upon them which is incurable, and each punishment is distinctly separate from the others."

And after three days a fearful judgment overtook them so that their agreement was shattered, they were humiliated, and their stiff necks broken. One of them was stricken with elephantiasis, until he was thoroughly diseased and putrid. Another, again, was swollen suddenly like a wine skin, and could not walk. They took him up to bring him to the Blessed One, and because he was unable to sit on an ass, as they were supporting him and he was creeping slowly along, he stumbled and fell, and his belly burst open, so that he died. And that other one, too, was smitten of an evil spirit, so that his mouth was contorted. He gnawed his tongue and arms and tore his garments. And bound in chains they brought him to the Saint. And after he was a long time in that affliction, they with difficulty persuaded the Blessed One in his behalf. Then he prayed for him, and he was restored a little, and came to himself and recounted before every one his acts of wickedness. When the Saint heard it, he said to him, "According to your deeds has God requited you. Because of this your punishment was without mercy."

CHAPTER XVIII

THE VISIONS OF MAR SIMEON

Concerning visions and revelations which appeared from God to the Blessed Mar Simeon, no one is capable of telling about them, or speaking of them. He, too, was very careful and fearful lest any one should think of him as though he told them in ostentation. But to those in whom he had confidence from time to time he spoke openly, making it known to them that it was not his wish that they should tell them to the public while he was living.

He saw one time a ladder placed on the earth, whose top reached the heavens. Three men stood upon it, one at its top, one midway of it, and one at its foot. A throne of majesty was set, and our Lord Jesus Christ himself sat there, while the hosts of heaven stood on his right and on his left, and a voice was heard calling by name that one who stood midway and saying to him, "Come up to me, and I will show thee." He went up until he came to him. And again a voice was heard which said, "This is Moses the great prophet, who received the law from God on Mount Sinai, and by whose hands miracles and signs were done. He became great in the sight of God and honored of all men, and another prophet like him did not arise in Israel after him. Thus also thou, if thou doest well and right, shalt be greater than all thy contemporaries. And as I was with Moses, so also will I be with thee." Then he gave him three keys.

And the Blessed Mar Simeon turned around and saw that one who stood at the foot of the ladder, and said, "Lord, who is this?"

And he heard a voice which said, "Call him and let him ascend and stand where thou art standing, for after thee he shall fill thy place." Then the saint called him three times, and he went up and stood where he was standing in the middle of the ladder.

Again, after these things, as he stood in prayer at noon, a vision appeared to him, marvellous and fearful. When he saw it he was afraid and trembled, alarmed, and covered his face with his cloak from fear. For he saw a chariot of fire with horses of flame and wheels of flame and reins of flashing rays, and its rug of blazing fire. A man sat upon it who came and stood before the saint as he was in the chariot, and said to him, "Be not afraid and be not affrighted, but be strong and valiant and brave, and of mortal man be not afraid. But rather above everything have care for the poor and the oppressed, and rebuke the oppressors and the rich. For lo, the Lord is thy helper, and there is no one who will harm or hurt thee. For thy name is written in the book of life, and a crown and honor are prepared for thee with all the Fathers, and with thy brethren the Apostles. For I am Elijah, he who in zeal shut up the heavens, and gave Ahab and Jezebel as food to the dogs, and slew the priests of Baal." When he said these things, he departed, mounting to heaven on the chariot.

But the Blessed One was greatly astounded at this vision, while he thought and pondered: "Who are those poor about whom command was given? The cripples who go about begging? The oppressed? Or those who live in monasteries, who for the sake of God left their people and their possessions and rest upon the hope of our Lord?"

And when he had been many days thinking and pondering about this vision, while he stood and prayed there appeared to him Mar Elijah a second time in the chariot of fire. And he drew near and stood before the saint and answered and said to him, "On what account is thy mind disquieted? Concerning that which I commanded about the poor? Thou shalt care equally therefore for all men, for the poor, and the injured and the monks who dwell upon the hope of our Lord. Have a care also for the priests, the churches, and the laws of God which are established, and see that no man treat with contempt or despise the commands of the priest. Deliver the oppressed from their oppressors, rescue the burdened from those who crush them, and uphold the rights of orphans and widows. Be not afraid and do not tremble and do not be terrified, neither before kings nor judges. Do not show favoritism to the rich. But openly rebuke them, and be not afraid of them, because they are not able to harm thee, just as were unable to harm me Ahab and Jezebel, when I decreed death upon them and gave their bodies as food to the fowls of the heaven. Let not thy mind therefore be disturbed, but possess thyself in patience and endurance, and do not let bodily afflictions seem irksome to thee." When Mar Elijah had commanded him again these things, he departed from him in his chariot.

CHAPTER XIX

THE PHYSICAL SUFFERINGS OF MAR SIMEON

Thereupon the holy Mar Simeon, after these visions and commands, was strengthened and encouraged and given resolution and animated; so he added to his former labor tenfold, and made himself a mandra, standing openly day and night while every one gazed at him. He deprived himself of food, so that not even that small amount he had taken would he have allowed himself to take after these visions, had they not persuaded him to take from time to time. For as he thought of those two men who were for a sign in his vision, Moses and Elijah, he said, "Oh that one would teach me and show me by what manner of conduct those two men attained all this greatness and this excellent glory! By faith? or charity? or humility? or chastity? or zeal?" For he was greatly perplexed by that vision and by that dignity. Also he continually questioned those who were versed in Scripture, that he might learn from them about their course of life. Some told him that it was in humility, and some told him, in charity, and some told him, in zeal. And it was not wearisome to that spiritual wisdom that it should humble itself to inquire even of the least.

And when he learned from many about their courses of life, he began to adopt them for himself, immoderate fasting, standing day and night, continual prayer, persistent supplication, godly zeal which burned like a fire in him, bodily chastity with purity of his members. For what tongue is there that dare attempt the narration concerning this man, who while he was in the flesh exhibited among men the deeds and acts of the spirit? For he stood like a strong man, and was valiant like an athlete, and endured with fortitude all sufferings, and held in contempt all diseases, and lightly esteemed the Evil One and defeated Satan and scattered his hosts and put to nought his army, and received the crown of victory. For he publicly fastened his feet upon a pillar, clothed mysteriously with heavenly power. The fleshly body of his feet burst open from standing, but his whole mind was kindled for his Lord. The joints of his vertebra were dislocated by continued supplication, but he strengthened his mind with love of Christ his Helper.[17]

He did not mind severe diseases of his body, for his mind was kindled towards his Lord all the time. He did not grow weary in distresses, and the billows which rolled over him all the time did not harm him, because his trust was stayed on his God. He was not afraid of his physical afflictions, and gave no enjoyment to his body even for one hour. His eyes were weak from vigils, but his mind was clear in the vision of his Lord. For he chose affliction rather than repose, trouble rather than rest, hunger rather than satiety. For he ardently desired that he might be in affliction in this world, for Christ's sake, that with him he might possess full enjoyment in the Holy City. For he endured such suffering, that neither among the ancients nor the moderns could be found any who had suffered as he did. For what body is there, or what limbs, that could endure with fortitude in such a manner?

For he stood forty years upon a pillar which was about a cubit in width. And his feet were bound and fettered as though in the stocks, so that neither to right nor left was he able to shift one of them, until even the bones and sinews of his feet were visible, from suffering. Also, his belly burst open from standing. And so his disciples used to say that the suffering of his belly was more severe than of his feet. Three of the joints of his spine were dislocated from that constant supplication with which he was bowing and lifting himself up straight again before his Lord, until he had completed his discipline. Also he lost his eye-sight forty days together while he stood upon the pillar, from fasting and vigil beyond measure. But no one knew it except his disciples. For his eyes were open and he talked with everyone, but he could not see. And when our Lord willed, and he completed the forty days, suddenly his sight was restored. And no stranger knew either that it was lost or restored, because he commanded his disciples that they should not tell any one.

These sufferings therefore he endured, the brave athlete. For he stood valiantly against the heat of the sun in summer, and against the severity of the cold in winter. Therefore the sun was like a crucible and that saint like gold. The fire therefore lowered its temperature, the furnace of testing grew cool, and the athlete of God came off victorious. For it says in Scripture, "Who can stand before his cold?"[18] For the north wind came with its snow, and the west with its ice, and the east with its gale, and the south with its sultriness; all of them combined together, accompanied also by heavy rain, and joined war with the wise master-builder who had built his house upon the rock. But the wind grew calm, the ice melted, and the rain was absorbed, and the Blessed One came off victor.

Who then is not astonished that he with his feet burst open, and his belly too, stood day and night! Wounded in body like Job, he was revived spiritually like him. For Job lay upon the dung heap, yet his prayer went up on high. Thus also the Blessed Mar Simeon, his feet fastened upon the pillar, but his prayer free and well-pleasing to his God. Then the illustrious Mar Simeon was slandered by Satan, like Job, before God, when he said, "Give me power over him, that I may enter into contest with him as I please." And when he received power over him on one of those days as he stood praying, a severe disease smote him in his left foot. While he was wishing for the evening to come, it was filled with ulcers; and when the next day dawned, it burst and emitted foul odor and was alive with maggots. Matter and a disgusting smell came from the foot, and maggots fell out of it upon the ground. So powerful and bad was the stench that not even half way up the ladder could one ascend except with distress. Some of his disciples who forced themselves to go up to him could not ascend until after they had put on their noses incense and fragrant ointment.

He suffered this way nine months until nothing was left of him except the breath only. And the report of his affliction was heard everywhere, even reaching kings. Bishops and periodeutes and many people came and tried to persuade him either to come down from the pillar until his disease was cured, or to take off one section from it, that it might be easier for a physician to go up to him and apply remedies to him; but he did not yield to persuasion. Even the victorious king Theodosius with his sisters[19] sent bishops to him for the sake of this, that they might persuade him to come down a little while. But the Blessed One, as became him, dismissed the bishops skillfully by saying, "You, indeed, pray for me. And I have confidence in my Lord Jesus Christ whom I serve, that he will not allow his servant to be humiliated to such a degree that he should come down from his position. For he knoweth how his worshipper hath entrusted himself to him, and he will not let me need physicians and herbs and medicines."

When eight months were completed lacking twenty days, and the disease was gaining so much the more strength, and the trouble growing worse, and it was now the beginning of Lent, when he was accustomed to shut the door, the priests of the villages and many people gathered in order to persuade him that he should not close the door of the enclosure, lest he should happen to depart from the world in this trouble and they be deprived of his blessing.

59

But the Saint said to them "Far be it from me, all the days of my life, that I should break the vow I have made to my God. But what is mine to do I will do, and what rests with Him His will shall accomplish. For whether I die or live, I am His."

When the door of the enclosure was shut and he had been in that affliction three days, his disciples thought the time of his departure was at hand, because he had entirely wasted away and nothing remained of him but his skeleton, and he was not able to speak. Being greatly grieved, they began to beseech and implore of him that he would bless them and commend them to our Lord. Thereupon the Saint, seeing them grieved and weeping, exerted himself and talked with them with much suffering, and comforted and consoled them and said to them, "Be not troubled. For I trust our Lord, whom I serve, that he will shortly give me deliverance."

And when he had been in seclusion thirty eight days, in the night between the third day of the week and the fourth, in that week in which the door of the mandra was opened, at midnight suddenly there was something like lightning, and the whole cell was lighted up by it. And there appeared to him in the likeness of a youth a beautiful one clothed in white, who stood before the Blessed One between earth and heaven. And he answered and said to him, "Fear not, but be strong and of good courage. For, lo, thy discipline is ended, thy slanderer put to shame, and thy crown prepared in heaven." And as he talked with him, he stretched out his hand and touched him on that foot of his from which he was suffering. At once the disease fled from it, his pain ceased, his body was invigorated, his countenance grew radiant, his face shone, he recovered his speech, and that foul disagreeable odor passed away. And when his disciples arose early to go up to him, they found him rejoicing and serene and praising our Lord. As though our Lord had made known to him what was about to happen, he had sent away the two of them when it was evening and had not permitted them to remain with him as usual. When therefore they arose early and saw him in such a radiant condition, and saw that his mind was calm and that the foul odor was turned to sweet fragrance, they begged and implored him to tell them how that disease was cured. And especially John his disciple urged him, because he loved him greatly and was constantly with him. And when he had urged him much, he pledged them not to tell anyone during his lifetime. Thereupon he told them how he was healed and what was said to him in that vision. For it was made known to him what was about to happen, and this he revealed to no one. But he was praying and groaning that he might depart from the world before that sign which was manifested to him should be fulfilled.

After the door of the mandra was opened, there assembled and came to him the bishops and elders and many people, and they saw him well and cheerful and seeking mercies from God. Then the good Mar Domnus[20] the Bishop of Antioch, went up with the disciple of the Saint and gave him the Eucharist. Then every one went away to his own place in peace, and the athlete continued in his ascetic practice, rejoicing and praising God.

CHAPTER XX

THE OPPRESSED ARE RELIEVED THROUGH THE AGENCY OF MAR SIMEON

But in one of those times a certain man who was a counselor seized the power that he might govern the city of Antioch. And he was a man evil and wicked, who oppressed and plundered many, but especially those who dyed skins red. He imposed upon them three times as much taxes as they had given in any year. So they came and informed the Saint; now they were about three hundred men; and they fell down before him. And when the Saint knew, he sent word to him, "This evil should not come through thee, that thou shouldst impose this burden upon these poor people and they should be required to bear it for ever. But be merciful to them and tax them as they were formerly accustomed to be taxed."

But he in his pride and stubbornness made answer to the one who was sent to him, "Go say to Simeon who sent thee, 'Give them thyself some of the gold which thou hast collected. For I, if I seize them, will imprison them, and not a thing will be left to them.'"

And when the saint learned these things, he lifted his eyes to heaven and said, "Lord, thou knowest that from the day I became a monk I have not taken for myself a coin,[21] and do not possess a thing except these skins with which I am clad; and lo, before God I am giving an account, But as for those who are thinking these things about me, Lord, forgive them."

After three days the appointed judgment overtook the wicked one, and an incurable disease devoured him. His belly swelled up like a wineskin, even while those poor people were in the mandra. Being in anguish, he wrote letters to the priests of some villages of his, that they should go up to beseech the Blessed One on his behalf. He also spent much money upon drugs and physicians, but no one could give him any help. And when those priests went up, and besought him much in his behalf, the Saint said to them, "Take some of this water and go. If God knows that when he is healed he will turn away from his evil deeds, mercy will be shown him and he will recover. But if he would continue in his wickedness, he will never see this water at all."

Taking the water they went, and as they arrived at the door of his dwelling, he asked that he might be turned over in his bed, whereupon on a sudden his belly burst open, and his bowels gushed out so that he died. So he did not see that water at all, according to the word of the Saint. And there was fear upon many, and the oppressed were delivered, and our Lord was glorified through his worshipper.

Again, there was a tribune of the empress in the north in the land of Nicopolis, who lived wickedly. He plundered and oppressed many and robbed orphans and widows of their substance, and the judgment of God was not before his eyes. They came and made it known to the Saint about his evil deeds. He sent a message to him: "Turn away from these deeds of which I hear concerning thee, and do not take by robbery that which is not thine, lest thou lose even that which is thine."

But he, impious, in his pride and arrogance was not satisfied to reject the word of the Saint, but seized him who was sent to him and heaped many insults upon him, saying to him, "Go show him who sent thee." That very day he was smitten with disease for which there was no cure, and withered up like wood, and a word never again went cut of his mouth, except this which he said, "Mar Simeon, have pity upon me," and immediately he expired. And they brought him and buried him, even while he who had been sent to him from the Saint was there.

One time it was rumored that men were murmuring because he wrote letters of persuasion to them in behalf of the poor and oppressed and orphans and widows who were treated with violence. And the Saint was troubled in his mind and said, "Sufficient for me is God, who knows that for the sake of helping their souls I persuade them to do good works. But henceforth, since this annoys them, I give the affair into the hands of God." So he commanded his disciples, and said to them, "Do not send anything to anyone, nor receive a thing from those who bring gifts, until

I see what the will of God is."

And after three months, in which the oppressed came there and no one listened to them, and others brought alms which no one received from them, so that both parties went away grieved, there appeared to the Saint a wonderful and fearful vision. As he prayed at midnight he saw two men whose aspect was very pleasant, and many people were with them one of them accused the Saint and said to him, "These are the commands which were enjoined upon thee: that thou shouldst be patient and longsuffering towards everyone, and so shouldst prosper and succeed. But thou—instead of this thou hast been impatient, and in the little while that humanity has pressed upon thee, whom I sent to thee, thou hast grown tired of them and hast restrained thyself from sending out a word in behalf of the oppressed and sorrowful and persecuted. Besides thou hast not received thankofferings from those who brought them in recognition of the saving of their lives. But since this is thy choice, I will take away from thee those keys which I gave thee, and another will receive them; and do thou continue as thou art."

But the other one, when he saw how greatly chagrined the Saint was, made entreaty for him and said, "I will pledge for him that he will do everything thou commandest him." And he approached and said to the Blessed One, "It is thine to say, and thy Lord knows what He will do."

Just after this vision there came to the Blessed One two youths, sons of a certain man who was a friend of the Saint, and made known to him that a certain Comes in Antioch, a wicked man, who held the government of the East, was making great misery for them in that he was seeking to bring them into the council, because of the enmity he had against their father, and so was trying to take revenge.[22] When the Saint learned it, he sent word to that wicked one, "Do not

64

harass and vex those boys, because they are mine."

But he, vile one, in mockery sent back word to the Blessed One: "If thou dost command me, I will carry filth after them and like a slave will wait on them."

When that wicked man heard that the door of the mandra was closed for the fast of forty days, he saw the boys as they entered the city, and seized them, taking from them pledges that they would enter and attend upon the council. They then sent their guardians with a certain attendant who was attached to them, who went and told the Saint these things. He sent word to him a second time: "I have said to thee, Keep thyself from those boys and do not harass them, lest harm befall thee, and no one will be able to give thee aid."

But that wicked and evil Pharaoh the second, in his pride and arrogance, could not conceal the deceit that lurked in his mind but showed his wickedness openly, and in the presence of his retinue said to the one who was sent to him from the Saint: "Go say to Simeon who sent thee, 'I hear that thou art shutting thyself up for forty days, and no one will enter thy dwelling or bother thee in that time. But take the trouble to curse me roundly during those days, for I do not desire that any of thy prayer should be inflicted on me.'" Which did indeed happen to him. The fool did not know that the justice of the Lord was already standing over him.

When the Saint heard this from the one who was sent, he shook his head and laughed softly to himself and said, "The simpleton! He hath sent word that all the forty days we should concern ourselves with him, and desist from the prayer in which we entreat God for our sins and for every creature; before one breath of the justice of the Lord can he stand? As for us, we counseled him that thing which we knew to be for his advantage. Since then he hath chosen for himself the curse rather than the blessing, the thing which he asketh from the Lord He will quickly grant him."

The Saint closed the door of his cell on the first day of the week, and one day only remained that vile one at peace; then a destined fearful judgment such as befitted his deeds overtook him. For they accused him before the king and the governor, when he was not aware, because of the wickedness which he did and because he harassed many. So five officers were sent after him, whose minds were more malignantly cruel than his. And on the third day of the week, in that first week of Lent, they seized him publicly in the forum as he was passing along in state. And they dragged him down from his chariot with great violence and unbelted him and, tearing off his toga from him, cast a rope about his feet and dragged him headlong, and so drew him along in a most unmerciful manner, because his humiliation was from the Lord. Then they threw him into irons, as had been commanded them.

Thereupon he sent and had those boys brought, against whom he had stood, and entreated them, saying, "Go beseech the Saint to write to the king in my behalf. For I know that all this has befallen me because I treated his command with contempt."

But they replied, "The Blessed One has closed the door of his cell, and is talking with no one except his Lord in prayer. But if the door of his cell were opened and he heard, then he would write to the king and the governor. For Mar Simeon is as compassionate as his Lord."

Then they led him away and brought him up with insulting treatment into all the cities on the route, and when they entered the royal city, there also he experienced great insult, all his property was plundered, and he was sent into exile. And as he was going on the way, he died a grievous death. So that curse which he had asked for followed him even to the day of his death.

CHAPTER XXI

THE PEOPLE ARE RESCUED FROM RODENTS
AND EVIL CREATURES BY THE PRAYERS
OF MAR SIMEON

Again, after the door of the Saint's cell was opened, there came there many people from the region of Aphshon, who made known to him about those large fieldmice and arnogs[23] which were lacerating live sheep and eating their entrails so that they died. They even leaped[24] upon the oxen and cattle, whereupon the animals would run until they were exhausted and fell; then they ate them. They had a way of grunting like swine, and would not flee from the presence of a man. Moreover they ventured up to small children and followed after them like dogs. And when the Saint heard, he was amazed and astounded, and marvelled and said, "No one can stand before the abominable vermin if it is given power; before the justice of the Lord who can stand?" But as they greatly besought him with tears and groans, he said to them, "Take some of this *ḥnāna* in the name of our Lord Jesus Christ, and make in every house three crosses, and on the four sides of every village make the sign of the cross; then keep vigil there and observe the Eucharist three days and entreat our Lord. I have confidence in God whom I worship, that on the third day not even one will be found there." So they went and did as he said to them, and on the third day no one knew what had happened to them, but it was as though the earth had opened its mouth and swallowed them up. And they turned away and went to their homes, praising our Lord who had shown loving kindness to them.

Again, there came to the holy Saint many people from Lebanon, who told him about some evil creatures which went out in all Mount Lebanon and were ravaging and attacking men and devouring them. And lamentations and mournings were resounding in all the mountain, for there was not a village there in which there had not been at least two or three people eaten every day. And sometimes, forsooth, they appeared as women whose hair was shaved, wandering about lamenting; and sometimes again as beasts. And they even entered into houses and seized people, and snatched infants from their mothers' breasts, and ate them before them, while they stood and looked on at their sucklings, unable to succor their own children, so that there was mourning and lamentation. Absolutely no one was able to go out to the field unless many went together armed with swords and staves. Not even under those circumstances would they get out of a man's way, except for a little way, and then again they would turn back into their tracks.

And when the holy Saint heard these things, he said to them, "God has rewarded you according to your deeds. For ye have forsaken him who made you in his goodness and feeds and cares for you in his mercy, and ye have taken refuge in dumb idols which have no profit in them, which do neither good nor evil. On this account God has delivered you over to the evil animals, which have taken vengeance on you. Go call now on those idols which ye worship; let them be your protectors and drive away from you this wrath which is sent upon you from God."

But they entered and prostrated themselves before his pillar with loud outcries; also many people who happened to be present implored him in their behalf. When the Saint saw how they were prostrated and supplicating, and that people besides were weeping and entreating, for their story was fit to bring tears, because their affliction was without mercy (for parents saw their children eaten up before them, and their limbs torn to pieces, and their corpses dragged away, and they could not help them), he said to them: "If indeed

68

ye forsake that error which possesses you, and turn to God your Creator and make a covenant that ye will be Christians and will receive baptism, then I will entreat the God whom I serve, that he may have mercy upon you and remove from you this rod of wrath which has come upon you."

And they all out of the agony of their hearts cried out as though with one mouth and said, "If thou prayest for us and this rod of wrath passeth away from us, we will covenant ourselves and bind ourselves in writing before thy holiness, that we will be Christians and receive baptism, and renounce idols and break down their shrines and smash their images. Only let this scourge pass away from us."

And when the holy master saw that they repented with all their heart, he said to them, "Take some of this *ḥnāna* in the name of Christ, and go, and on the borders of each village set up four stones; and if there are elders there, call them, and upon each stone make three signs of the cross, and keep vigil there three days. Then ye shall see the sign which God will do, because never again will they destroy the likeness of man there." Which thing God did really do. For they went and found that from that very time when the Saint prayed, not one of them ever again entered a village, neither had power to hurt a man; but they went and came in the fields, but did not enter the villages, and were not molesting[25] any one. For as though the command of heaven was upon them, thus they seemed.

And after they went and did as the holy master said to them, there was there a great sign and marvellous wonder. For there came from all that region men, women, and children without number, and receiving baptism they became Christians and turned to God from that vain superstition. And they told before him: "After we went and set up those stones and made the cross upon them, as thy holiness commanded, and those three days of vigil passed away, we saw forsooth, those animals going and coming and walking around those stones and howling; and their howling was loud upon the mountain. Then some of them fell down and burst open as they stood beside those stones, and some of them, again, went away howling. And, forsooth, by night their howls were heard like the sound of women wailing and crying out and saying, 'Woe upon thee, Simeon, what hast thou done to us!'" And they brought those three with them the pelts of three of them, and they hung on the door of the mandra a long time. And those skins were not like leopards', nor bears', but the colors were various. They continued about ten days in that howling and wailing, and some died, and of the rest not even one could be found by searching.

And the people of that region, after they received baptism and became Christians, remained in the mandra of the Saint about one week; then they went away to their houses rejoicing and praising and blessing God, who had shown loving kindness to them. And from that time they failed not to come and go to the Saint and receive baptism, they and their children. And this was for the advantage and wellbeing of their souls.[26]

CHAPTER XXII

A DRY SPRING IS RESTORED THROUGH THE PRAYERS OF MAR SIMEON

Again, there was a large spring in the vicinity of Ganadris in a certain village, which watered many fields. And suddenly it failed and dried up and ceased its flow, so that the trees withered and whatever was sown by them among their watercourses completely failed. And they fetched workmen who digged and delved, but all to no purpose. Then at last they were compelled to come and tell him concerning what they had done. For the Saint had issued an order that on the first day of the week no workman should work until the evening. But one of them dared to go irrigate on the first day of the week, at dawn, and when they saw it, instead of stopping him or hindering him, as though the thing pleased them they all scattered, went out and left the church, and each one of them went to his own quarter to irrigate. And after evening came on they left the fountain full and gushing. Then they arose early in the morning seeking in it at least one drop of water, but there was none. And this from which they had drunk on the first day of the week was hot and dry as though a fire smouldered in it. And when they saw, they smote their faces with their hands, because of what had happened to them in their presumption. So when they had toiled and employed every device, and no help came from any quarter, they were compelled to come and tell the Saint. As soon as he heard their confused stories, he knew and understood and said to them, "This appears to me to be a case of law-breaking."

Seeing that they were detected, they told him the affair just as it really was and as it happened. And when the Saint knew, he was exceedingly enraged at them and scolded them severely, and ordered that they drive them out of his presence with violence and blows. For he was blazing like fire with zeal for his Lord. And when they went out from him, they cast themselves down and fell prostrate by the outer door of the mandra, and lay three days beseeching and imploring everyone who entered or went out that he would try to persuade the Saint for them. And their elder went and brought elders and other periodeutes and tried to persuade his Holiness. He learned that they had indeed been at the door three days, and his compassion was manifested upon them, and he gave commandment, and they entered his presence, Then he said to them, "I advise you for your own salvation. For neither gold nor silver am I seeking for you, but your souls, that I may establish them before God in confidence."

And when they entered, they confessed their folly and made an agreement in writing that they would never do the like of this again. He said to them, "In the name of our Lord Jesus Christ take three chips and make upon them crosses and throw them into the fountain where it springs out. And take *ḥnāna* and make three signs of the cross on this side and on that; then go in, keep vigil in the church. At dawn, arise, see what our Lord has done."

So they went and did as he said to them, and arose at dawn and found the fields all overflowed and the fountain full and spouting forth three times as much as formerly. Then they all came in a crowd; and, praising and blessing God who did this loving kindness for them, they went away in peace rejoicing.

CHAPTER XXIII
THE MIRACLES ACCOMPLISHED BY MAR SIMEON OVER GREAT DISTANCES

These things, then, and more than these our Lord performed through the saint Mar Simeon. For what mouth can speak or tell about the signs and heroic exploits which our Lord did through him, not only in the neighborhood but also at a distance, both on sea and among the heathen and among Magi who worship fire and water. And really, I think, in the case of the Saint was fulfilled that which our Lord spoke in his Gospel: "Those who believe in me, the works that I do shall they do."[27] For it is written concerning Simon Peter,[28] that his shadow as he passed by overshadowed the sick and they were healed, and it fell upon such as were very ill and they recovered. And again[29] concerning the apostle Paul, that his girdle or his handkerchief they took and, going, put upon such as were smitten by the Enemy, and they recovered; and upon the sick who were ill of obstinate diseases, and they were delivered from their afflictions. But Mar Simeon the Blessed, while he was indeed their spiritual brother and disciple, greatly admiring their labors and following in their footsteps, with his soul exulting every time he heard of their heroic deeds, yet was one whose measure extended very far above that of all other men. For he did not walk upon the earth that his shadow might fall upon any one, nor was aught of his clothing sent to the sick at any place; but only words of prayer proceeded out of his mouth and went to far-away places, and his Lord wrought healing and recovery.

About those things which I said that our Lord did through him and through his prayer in distant places and on the sea and among the heathen, a little from much we will narrate. For they are many; and who is able to speak or tell about them? The treasury of Christians is a great ocean whose breadth is immeasurable and its depth unfathomable. For as one who fills a bottle from the ocean or takes a spoonful out of the Euphrates or lifts up a grain from the sand, without diminishing their quantity or lessening their number; thus also whoever draws out and takes, is satisfied with the gift of the spirit which the servants of God receive from their Lord. For He is rich, and they suffer no poverty. For, few of the many heroic acts of the faithful are written, for the benefit of humanity, and as the ear can receive. For they resemble their Lord in their activities, who follow in the footsteps of their Lord, him of whom said the Evangelist in wonder and astonishment, as he saw the deeds and works of his unnumbered mercies, which can not be reckoned up: "If one by one were written those things which did our Lord Jesus Christ, the world would not contain the books which should be written."[30]

As for the holy Mar Simeon, then, since your ear loves to hear of his illustrious deeds, and more sweet to you than honey to those who eat it is the story of the beautiful deeds which our Lord did through his athlete; little from much, dear Sir, from the treasury of the splendid acts of the Blessed One we are telling before you—those things which we saw with our eyes and handled with our hands; and these also which happened at a distance, and were written by faithful men to the saint.

For there came to him Antiochus bar Sabinus, made prefect of Damascus, and said to his Holiness before every one: "Naaman came up to that desert which is near Damascus, and made a feast and invited me. For at that time there was not yet enmity between him and the Romans. While we were sitting at meat, he introduced the subject of Mar Simeon and said to me, 'This one whom you call Mar Simeon, is he a god?'

"And I said to him, 'No, he is not a god, but he is the servant of God.'

"Again Naaman said to me, 'When the report about Mar Simeon was heard among us, and some of our Arabs began to go up to him, some chiefs of my camp came and said to me, "If thou allowest them to go up to him, they are going to be Christians and will follow the Romans and rebel against thee and leave thee." Then I sent and called together all my camp and said to them, "If any one dares to go up to Mar Simeon, I will take off his head and the heads of all his tribe, with the sword."

"'When I had spoken and commanded them and had let them go, at midnight as I lay in the tent I saw a certain man of splendid appearance, the like of whom I had not seen; and there were five others with him. When I saw him, my heart failed, and my knees quaked, and I fell down and worshipped him. But he indignantly returned a severe answer to me, saying, "Who art thou, that thou dost restrain the people of God from the house of God's servant?" Then he commanded those four, and they stretched me out by my hands and feet, and that other one gave me a severe and cruel beating. There was no one to rescue me from his hands, until he had compassion upon me and gave command; whereupon they released me. Then he drew the sword which he was carrying and showed it to me and swore to me with solemn oaths, "If again thou darest to hinder even one person from prayer in the house of Mar Simeon, with this sword I will cut off thy limbs and those of all thy tribe."

"'I arose in the morning and assembled all the tribe and said to them, "Whoever wishes to go up to the house of Mar Simeon and there receive baptism and be a Christian, let him go safely and without fear."'

"And moreover Naaman said to me, 'If I were not a subject of the King of Persia, I also would go up to him and would be a Christian. By reason of that fright and beating, for more than a month I was unable to rise and go out of doors. And lo, I commanded, and there are churches, bishops, and elders in my camp. And I said, "Whoever wishes to be a Christian, may be without fear. And whoever desires to be a heathen, this again is his privilege."'"

And everyone who heard as it was told, gave glory to God, who was so enlarging the fame of his worshippers everywhere.

Again, a certain Magian among the Persians, chief of all the Magi, even he who was chief of all that wickedness, entered the presence of that one who was called "King of Kings", and power was given to him over the Christians, whom they called Nazarenes, that he might oppress and beat and imprison and chastise them as he pleased, in order to make them renounce their religion. Those who stood steadfast and did not apostatize, he had power to send out of the world by cruel tortures and painful deaths. And when this wicked and vile one received the power over the flock of Christ, like a shameless wolf without mercy, the enemy of the Lord[31] seized and bound and flogged and beat many people, men and women, elders and monks, and laymen besides, not a few, them and their wives and their children, and inflicted many torments upon them and passed sentences of torments of all kinds, like a man who did not have the judgment of God before his eyes; and the wicked one knew not that the just judgment of the Most High would quickly overtake him. For after he had tortured them as he pleased, with all tortures and torments, he seized and bound about three hundred and fifty of them, and threw on them irons and chains and fetters, and imprisoned them all together in a dark house. Then he set guards over them, so that no one should give them bread or water, but that thus they might die of hunger and thirst.

But after they had been in this misery about ten days and there was no one to have compassion on them and deliver them, as they prayed they said in prayer, "O God, to whom all these things are easy, at the prayers of Mar Simeon Thy worshipper according to Thy divine pleasure, let there be deliverance to the souls that take refuge in Thee. And let not these vile heathen say, 'The Christians have no God.'" While they prayed and all together made supplication, at midnight our Lord did a great miracle before them. The Saint appeared to them, standing on the pillar, and stood among them, and a great light was with him, and blazing torches, and he was clothed in white skins, and his face seemed like lightning, and he said to them, "Peace be with you, my brethren. I am Simeon, your brother, he who stands upon the pillar in the land of the Romans." Then he descended and greeted them and said to them, "Be strengthened and of good courage, neither let your minds be affrighted nor your hearts be troubled. For lo, your trial is ended, and your crown is prepared and kept in heaven before your Lord. You have two days more to be here; then on the third day you shall be released and go out in honor and triumph, and persecution shall cease and stop from the people of God, and his church. Even today a fearful judgment will overtake your enemy, and an affliction without mercy smite him. As he is exalted so shall he be humbled, and all the East be aware of his stroke."

Having spoken thus to them, again he was found standing on the pillar in the same manner in which he entered among them, and he floated away vanishing from their midst. But their great misery was alleviated after they had seen the Blessed One, so that indeed they were thinking that they were not even in prison.

But he, the illustrious Mar Simeon, went to that impious one in fearful apparition and indignant countenance, as he stood on his pillar, and there were with him torches like lightning. And when the wicked one saw him, his heart trembled and his knees shook, and his spinal joints were loosened, and his color turned to pallor, and he was like a dead man. He talked to him indignantly and terribly, and said to him, "Most vile and abominable of all men, art thou trying to oppose thyself to the name of the Lord God, and hast thou received authority over his servants, to oppress and scourge, and compel them to apostatize? Lo, now, quickly will overtake thee the justice of the Almighty; and who will be able to deliver thee or set thee loose from His hands?" When he had spoken to him these angry words, on a sudden there was something like a flash of lightning, and it smote that evil man so that it threw him down on his face. And a raging fire was kindled in him, and his whole body burned, and the smell of his burning went a great distance.

Then Mar Simeon said to him, "These documents which thou hast received from the king, send back to him. And send him word, 'Thus saith Mar Simeon, who standeth on a pillar in the land of the Romans: if thou dost not send and fetch out all the servants of God who are in prison, and let persecution of the church of Christ cease and come to a stop at thy command and through thy written documents'—, then I will bring upon him after three days something more severe than this judgment of thine." And when the holy Saint had said these things to him, he was taken up and ascended from his presence. As for the wicked man, he fell down crying out with shrieks because of that judgment, severe and bitter, which had seized him.

At the sound of his howling many people collected, and when they saw him in that severe merciless pain, they quaked and feared. And when they asked him what had happened to him, he said to them, "Simeon, that Christian who stands on a pillar in the land of the Romans, has treated me thus, because I persecuted the adherents of his faith. He said to me, moreover, 'Thou worshippest the fire, so in the fire will I burn thee; we will see if it will come to thine aid.' He commanded me, too, that those documents which I received from the King concerning the Christians, I should send back to him, and send him word, 'Command that all the Christians who are persecuted and imprisoned be released.' And thus he said to me, 'Unless he shall give orders and they go out inside of two days, and there be peace upon the Christians' church, a judgment more cruel and painful than this of thine I will bring upon him.'"

And he who is called "King of Kings," when he received the letters and learned from several people about the suffering and pain, cruel and severe, of that impious one, immediately issued orders, and all the incarcerated Christians were set at liberty, and the churches also that had been closed were opened. A manifesto was issued and posted in villages and cities of the Nazarenes, that no one should say a harmful word to them; but they should practice their worship according to former custom, without let or hindrance.

And bishops and elders who were far away and were not aware of what had happened, when they saw that on a sudden the command had gone forth, were astonished. And when those who had been imprisoned were released and had gone forth with great honor, and they learned from them how the Saint had appeared to them, and how he talked with them, and that all he said to them had proven true and had been realized, and they heard also of the affliction and severe judgment of that vile and wicked man, they praised and blessed God. And being all assembled together, they recorded the facts in writing and sent it to the Saint, by three elders from that place; and it was read many times before them. They were with the Saint two weeks; then they returned to their home blessing and praising God.

But the wicked man was in that distress, tormented with fire and consumed by worms, about ten days. Thus he died a death evil and distressing, and there was fear and terror upon all who beheld it. On account of it many turned to the fear of God, and becoming Christians received baptism.

And again, on the sea many times the Saint appeared manifestly to many sailors and helped them in their distresses in the time of danger, when storms and tempests arose against them. And they came and told him how they saw him plainly in the time when they were in peril, when immediately, as soon as he appeared, the sea grew calm, the waves were stilled, and the tempests were quieted. The Saint was much concerned, moreover, for the affairs of those who sail on the sea.

Now one time it happened that a certain large ship was

going down from Arabia from the upper district, and there were in it many people both men and women who were going down to their homes in Syria. Having embarked, they had gone half the journey, when the waves became stirred up, a violent wind raged, darkness fell upon them, and the ship was near to capsizing. For they would mount up to the sky, as it is written, and would descend into the abyss.[32] And as they cried out and were distressed and supplicated with tears and groans, and there was no help nor deliverance from any quarter, every one covered himself and fell upon his face, that he might not see death approaching. For they felt sure that they should never see dry land again, especially because they saw a man who was black and looked like an Indian,[33] who came and stood on the top of the mast which stood amidships. For it was said of him that every time he was seen in a ship he sank her.

When every one had given up hope of his life and believed he would die, and prostrate and wailing they had covered their faces, there was a man there from the village Aṭma, which is beside Āmēs[34] who had with him a little of the Saint's *ḥnāna*. And our Lord willed and put it in his mind that he might show a miracle by his worshipper and give deliverance to those endangered souls by the hand of his believer. So he recollected, and standing up and taking that *ḥnāna*, he made the sign of the cross with it on the mast which stood amidships, and rubbed handfuls of it on both sides of the ship while all the prostrate people cried out, "Mar Simeon, entreat thy Lord and help us by thy prayers!"

Immediately the Saint appeared, holding a scourge in his right hand. And he went up and stood on the top of the mast and seized the Indian by his hair and held him out and whipped him with the scourge, while the sound of his howling echoed over all the sea. And when he had scourged him severely and let him go, he fled still howling, as though many were pursuing him. And as he fled, thus he cried: "Woe to thee, Simeon! It is not enough for thee that thou dost banish me from the land, but lo, from the sea as well thou art driving me. Now where shall I go?"

And from the time the Saint appeared to them, the waves were calm, the tempest ceased, the air was clear, and the sea was quiet from its commotion. The Saint said to them, "Fear not, for you shall suffer no harm"; then he vanished from them. And from that time the wind was fair for them, and they proceeded on their voyage quietly without fear, until, our Lord willing, they entered the haven. And many clave to the one from Aṭma and came to the mandra of the Saint, where they recounted those things before him and before everybody. And every one who heard it blessed God, who had shown loving kindness to them and saved them at the prayer of his believer.[35]

Again, another ship was in port in Cyprus, loaded and full of much cargo, ready to sail to the west with many passengers and sailors on board, and some who were about to go up for trade; when suddenly a whirlwind came on, it grew dark, and the wind blew a gale, and entering into the ship, like the whirlwind which it was, lifted it from among its fellows, and it went up spinning around as far as the eye could see, like a stone slung by an engine; those who were in it wailing, and those outside of it crying out for help. It was indeed matter for groans and tears. For if it came down in the sea, it would sink and never be seen again. And if, on the other hand, it fell outside on the land, it would be broken to shivers, and all the people who were in it would be killed.

When they saw that it was all up with them, and help there was none unless the mercy of God willed it, they began to cry out and pray, saying, "Oh, Saint Simeon, help us by thy prayers!" And lo, once more, immediately the Saint appeared, standing beside the ship and encouraging those who were in it. And stretching out his right hand he seized hold of the ship and thus safely and gently brought her down, and drawing her along brought her and set her upright in the sea just inside the harbor, as one would take hold of a light thing. And the ship received not a particle of damage, and neither did the people in her. And when the ship came down and was standing in her place, those disturbances and whirlwinds became quiet. Many saw the Saint, besides those who were on board the ship. And they told it before everyone, how he encouraged them as he stood by them. And all who saw and heard those things which were told gave glory to God.

And when the master of the ship saw this great miracle which was performed, he took five of the sailors who were on board the ship, and came to the holy Saint, to whom they recounted those things before everyone. He said to him, moreover, "If thy Holiness commands me to journey by sea, at thy command, sir, I will sail. But if not, I will never embark again. But I will go sell the ship and will not seek the wealth of sea-trade."

Then the holy Saint said to him, "Take some of this *ḥnāna* in the name of our Lord Jesus Christ, and go make the sign of the cross three times on the ship and set sail. And I have hope in my Lord that He will accompany thee, and thou wilt go in safety and return prosperously." And all as many as heard when it was told were astounded and amazed and praised and blessed our Lord, who did in such wise the will of his worshipper.

Again, there was a certain maiden in the Persian domain, the daughter of a Christian, and she was beautiful to see and of comely appearance. More than her external appearance her mind was beautiful and excellent and charming, and acceptable to God. And one of the accursed fire-worshippers saw her, a basilisk who had the title of Marzevān, and he lusted after her to take her as one of his wives. For the girl, though a Christian, did not belong to any religious order. But when he sent to her parents many times, she neither gave heed to those who came nor gave them answer. For she said, "God forbid that I should go up to the bed of a vile man who worships the fire."

Therefore he went and sought to get her by an order from him whom they called "King of Kings." Then seeing that she did not obey it, he seized her by force, with many people, as though by command of the "King of Kings." And when she remained constant to her resolve and said, "Though I die, I will not go up with thee to the bed, for I am the virgin of Christ," he scourged her and shutting her up inflicted severe and bitter tortures upon her. And as she stood by her first resolve and said, "Though I die, with thee to bed I will not go up," and he was ashamed to have her flout him, thereupon he commanded his menials to hang a great stone weight on her neck and throw her into the river at the confluence of the Euphrates and Tigris. And as they took her out to throw her in, she raised her eyes to heaven and said, "O God of Saint Simeon, do Thou help Thy maidservant and see that for Thy name's sake I am about to die, because I will not defile myself in the bed of the unclean and abominable man who denies Thy name and worships dead idols." They put the weight on her and threw her into the river.

At the very moment she fell, the Saint was there standing in the midst of the river, and reaching out his hand grasped her and drew her out and fetched her up out of the river and stood her on the dry land, Then he loosed the weight from her and said to her, "Fear not, my daughter. The God in whose name thou believest is thy deliverer. As for that vile heathen, lo, the right hand of the Lord will smite him with an incurable disease." And he lead her and brought her as far as the edge of her village holding her by her right hand, while he exhorted her not to fear. When she reached her village he said to her, "My daughter, go in peace, and may the Lord be with thee."

Then she entered, and her parents saw her, they who were sitting in great grief and mourning on her account, and they were amazed and trembled and were astonished. And when they asked her by what means she came, she told them everything as it had happened, and how the Saint drew her out and brought her up from the river and conducted her as far as the border of her village, and all he said to her, and how suddenly he vanished from before her eyes when she reached the edge of the village.

As she was telling her parents, many gathered at sight of her, and lo, on a sudden the sound of violent weeping went up from the house of that wicked man who had seized her. For as he reclined and dined, and his servants were standing and waiting on him, and he was thinking how he would vent his spite on the parents of the girl as well, a fearful judgment overtook him. For as he reclined he saw a terrible man enter and draw his sword. And when he saw him, he was terrified and affrighted. He leaped to stand in front of him, and struck him on the head with the sword. Immediately his whole right side withered from his head to his toes, and he cried out violently with a loud voice and said, "Because I persecuted the maidservant of the God of the Christians it has happened to me thus; woe to him whoever assails or opposes Him!" And he never spoke another sentence, but lay in that great affliction, tortured, suffering, and worn out, prostrate like a dried-up tree, and he became a source of terror to those who beheld him. Because of his experience many of the heathen were afraid and terrified, and refrained from persecuting or harassing the Christians.

Then the father of the maid took the trouble to go up with many of the citizens of his place to the mandra of the Saint. And he told these things in the presence of the blessed St. Simeon before everyone. And all those who heard as he recounted, gave praise to God. And the father of the girl and the people of the village stayed with the Saint a week, when, having received his blessing, they turned back in peace, rejoicing and praising and blessing God.

CHAPTER XXIV

DROUGHTS ENDED THROUGH THE INTERCESSION OF MAR SIMEON

These things then and many besides our Lord did through his athlete. Also, rain was restrained many times; whereupon they assembled and coming to him besought him. He then supplicated his Lord, and He did His will so that there was rain, and worn out souls were refreshed and confessed and praised God and went down from his mandra rejoicing.

One time there was a great lack of rain; the whole winter passed, and Lent was now about to begin, yet not a drop of rain had fallen. Everybody prayed and made supplication, for the whole region of Beth Gubbē[36] was exhausted by drought. And to the mandra of the Saint every day came the priests, covered with sackcloth, their heads sprinkled with ashes, and their flocks with them, with tears and groanings. So they continued in that drought, while daily all creation was bowing down in the mandra of the Saint; yet there was no relief from any quarter. The winter now was about past and Lent therefore just commencing, when the Saint closed the door of his mandra. There happened to be there a certain procurator who had been very constantly in the mandra, and he loved, too, the disciples of the Saint. Being a man who had great freedom of speech with them, he said to them jokingly, as they stood talking together, "It is written that Elijah prayed and his Lord did his will, so that there was rain. Samuel also prayed in harvest, and his Lord answered, and there was rain in harvest. But today perhaps there is no one whose will his Lord will do as he did for those ancients. For, lo! how long a time all creation is tormented; yet no help comes from anywhere." When prayer was finished, and everyone went to his task, those disciples of the Saint drew near and told these things and said to him, "Thus did Ḳuriaḳos the procurator say to us."

But the Saint, when he heard these things from these his disciples, was confounded greatly and said to them, "I take oath that up to this time I have not prayed before my Lord that there should be rain upon the earth, because I see their rebellious deeds. But now that the Evil One hath sown this seed in their minds, send men everywhere and summon the priests with their flocks."

But the disciples of the blessed Saint Simeon drew near and used entreaty and said to him, "Lo, every day crowds fill the mandra. Now take heed lest any should be offended and they should say, 'Behold, he is sending and gathering together the world for the sake of his aggrandizement.' If thy Holiness knows that anything will happen,—but if not, send them away about their own affairs; lo, they come and go daily of their own accord."

But he said to his disciples, "Do you assemble them, and as for that which our Lord will do, it is not for you to worry about it. Do you carry out that which is commanded you, and my Lord knows what He will perform for the honor of His name." Thereupon they sent out and summoned them to come on Friday, and many people gathered there, a countless multitude. The mountains were covered, and the mandra was filled inside and out with men and women.

They also brought in small children who were learning the letters and placed them before the Saint, and their teachers sang antiphonally with them in the Greek language "Kyrie eleison," which is interpreted, "Lord, have mercy upon us."

Now the blessed Saint, when he saw the priests with ashes sprinkled on their heads, standing in sorrow and in anxiety, while the cries of men and women within and without ascended on high, and those children, too, like innocent lambs, and moreover the sun as hot as in summer, he was greatly grieved, his soul was moved and his compassion grew fervent. After he had prayed and made supplication before his Lord a long time, he raised his eyes to heaven and sighed and smote upon his heart with his hand three times, inside of his kasoula.[37] Then again clasping his hands behind him he bowed himself with his face upon his knees and remained bowed a long time. All the people too were praying that his Lord might do the will of his believer, As he bowed and prayed, everyone also standing in grief and tears, they looked to see what our Lord would do; when, lo, on a sudden there appeared some mist of white cloud. Thunder too, deep-toned, resounded after it and spread to every side; until the whole heavens were filled with it, and the wind blew violently.

Then the rain began to fall heavily, and it was also very cold. And all the people, who a little while before had been running to the shade from the extreme heat, took to flight for shelter from the wind and cold and heavy rain. And when the blessed Saint heard the sound of the water which was coming down into the cisterns as he bowed in prayer, and the voice of the people who were praising and blessing God for what they had seen, he raised himself up from the position of bowing in prayer, while his face shone like the rays of the sun, and his mind exulted and rejoiced that his

Lord had done his will.

And when he saw those who huddled together under shelter from the cold and rain, he called them and said to them, "A little while ago ye were weeping for rain, and now, behold, ye run from it." And he encouraged them and comforted them and said to them, "See, the Lord hath given you rain; and I trust in him and his goodness, that if ye walk uprightly, fearing him with all your hearts, keeping his laws and commandments, this year, although the winter is past, and ye have come to the conclusion that no one will reap a harvest, the Lord God will bless, so that its production will be two fold, and ye eat and be satisfied and bless the name of the Lord God." So he sent them away from him rejoicing, confessing and adoring and praising God. And there was rain again and many showers, and the year was blessed, as the Saint told them. And they filled the granaries with twice as much as the usual produce and gathered in large crops and filled their houses with the fruits of the earth. And they ate and were satisfied, and blessed and praised God their Sustainer.

Then after everyone was dismissed in peace from the presence of the Saint to his own place and dwelling, when evening came and the holy man remained with these disciples who ministered to him, they drew near, the two of them prostrating themselves before the Saint, and besought him with entreaty to reveal and show them in what manner he made the petition, or what he said in his prayer when he prayed and made supplication and entreated his Lord. But he was reluctant and declined to reveal or say either what he said or saw and heard. Again they persuaded him very earnestly. Then, solemnly adjuring them to tell no one during his lifetime, he revealed it to them and said, "When I saw these priests present with their flocks, their heads sprinkled with ashes, and all the people crying and these children pleading for help, I was grieved and troubled even to death. And to my Lord in prayer I said this: 'O Lord God, merciful and compassionate, either have mercy and relieve these afflicted souls who cry to Thee, who are assembled on account of Thy name, or take the life of Thy servant and never again let me see the distress of Thy people and Thy servants.' After this, while I bowed and my tears fell I saw a beautiful youth who came passing in front of me and said to me, 'Thy prayer is heard, thy petition accepted, thy wish accomplished, and thy request granted.' And at the time he spoke to me and passed before me, I heard the sound of the thunder booming and the sound of the wind blowing and the rain falling. Then I praised and blessed God, that he did not turn away from the prayer of His servant."

CHAPTER XXV

PROOFS THAT MAR SIMEON WAS CALLED TO STAND UPON HIS PILLAR BY GOD

These things then, and ten times more than these signs and wonders our Lord did through the blessed Saint Simeon. For we said before that there is no one of mortal men who could enumerate or count the benefits and deliverances which God wrought through him for men. Or who, again, is able to say and recount the wonderful things which were done by his prayers in distant places? And also many visions our Lord revealed and made known to him, a multitude of which he concealed, and did not speak of to any one; because he was careful that no one should think of him that he repeated them for his own glory. About this also a revelation was made to him. For he saw two men standing before him in fair and excellent garments, talking about this matter. One of them said to his companion, "See how many visions and revelations are shown to him, which he has concealed and hidden, and not revealed one of them to any one."

Thereupon the other one answered his companion, "He does very rightly. For this also he is to be commended, because he does not reveal and tell that which is shown to him from God for his encouragement. For by this it is evident that he does not seek his own glory, and there is no more any opportunity for others to speak the thing they desire."

When they had discussed with each other these things and many more than these, as they were walking to and fro in the mandra, they disappeared. They did not say anything to the Saint about this. He held his peace and they said nothing to him, but he knew that they said it as a caution. As a result of this he was extremely careful and refrained from repeating or saying anything about that which was revealed to him from God.

As for the monastic life and labor and practice, which he led and endured and suffered before God secretly and openly, this was evident and manifest to all men: that neither among the ancients nor the moderns was there a mortal body that could endure for one hour and withstand the hardships which the body of the blessed Saint Simeon bore and withstood. For we all know and are persuaded that for wonder and marvel the Holy Spirit wrote down the glorious deeds of believers in Holy Scripture for the comfort and encouragement and help and warning of humanity. For Moses, the great prophet, the clear-seeing eye of all Israel, the glorious athlete, the wise master-builder, the profitable servant, the vigilant mariner, the skilful pilot, the practiced scribe, the prince of the believing house, twice alone fasted forty days and forty nights, each time without eating bread or drinking water, while he was on the mount with his Lord, a cloud around, thick darkness encompassing, fire burning, smoke ascending, horns sounding, trumpets blaring, angels in trepidation, the watchers of Heaven alarmed, the holy angels and cherubim shouting, while Moses was talking and God answering him with the voice.[38] And he was refreshed, and his food was the divine vision, and his drink the heavenly splendor. He fared sumptuously in the fast and was purified in prayer.

Elijah, too, the zealot, the consuming fire, in the strength of that food which he received from the angel at the command of his Lord, which no one had sown and no one had provided, went forty days and forty nights and came to the mount and entered the cave. By the fast of forty days he was made worthy to hear the divine voice and see that fearful vision at which heavenly beings tremble and earthly beings are terrified; then he was sent to anoint kings and prophets. And he received thence the earnest of his fast, that from the world of sorrows he should be translated and taken up to Eden which is filled with all manner of delights.

Daniel, also, a man to be loved, scion of the household of faith, fasted twenty one days without eating bread or drinking water, and neither washed nor anointed himself; and a watcher from heaven, prince of the angels, was sent to him, and for his fasting and prayer revealed to him secrets and made known to him the future, and brought back the captivity from Babylon. By his fasting and prayer the seed of Abraham, the friend of God, were delivered from subjection to their enemies.

And we worship our Lord for his goodness, that His compassion upon the creation of His hands was kindled, and His mercy constrained Him, and coming down he wove and clothed Himself with the garment of flesh which He in His goodness had formed with His holy hands as seemed good to Himself; when He went out to the wilderness that He might be tempted, it is written that for forty days and forty nights He remained in fasting and prayer, not eating bread nor drinking water. As much as His divinity knew that the flesh of mortals can endure, so much it permitted the holy flesh which it had assumed to endure. And after the forty days in which He continued in fasting and prayer, it seemed good to His divinity and He beckoned to hunger and it came; and when He commanded, it approached Him, that He might make known and show that truly indeed He had assumed the flesh of Adam, that He might be subject to hunger and thirst and weariness and sleep. And in that flesh He overcame His enemy by fasting, and put Satan to confusion and scattered his hosts, trampled sin under foot, slew death, desolated Sheol, and received the crown of victory.

If then, as we have said, our Lord performed such wonders and signs through these mighty and wonderful men, by their fasting forty days at a time, what should we say about the blessed Saint Simeon, of whom no one can tell his ascetic practices, unless it is God who knows and is acquainted with his toil and his service! For he wearied himself and struggled and toiled before his God in mighty fasts untold, and in mighty prayers unconquerable. In hunger and thirst, in heat and cold, continually, unceasingly, in supplication without interruption, and standing at all times; who gave no sleep to his eyes nor repose to his body fifty-six years night and day. For he was in the monastery nine years, in wonderful discipline and severe practices, as we have written down and recorded above.

Then in the mandra besides, in Telneshē, he remained forty-seven years. He stood in a corner in the mandra ten years, some of the time in a cell, in great struggle and in contest and conflict with the Enemy. After these things he stood upon those smaller pillars seven years: on one of eleven cubits, on one of seventeen cubits, and on one of twenty-two cubits. And on that one of forty cubits he stood thirty years, while our Lord gave him strength and endurance so that on this he finished the days of his life in peace and tranquillity, with deeds of beneficence.

He had the good end with men of peace,[39] and his end was ten fold greater than his beginning. His Lord did his will and pleasure and granted his request. He asked and received. He knocked at the door of his Lord in truth, and it was opened unto him. For he honored God with a perfect heart, and was honored by God with all these rewards. He loved his Lord with all his heart, more than himself and his life; for he surrendered his soul and put it into the hands of his Lord. So his Lord, who saw his diligence, gave him favor in the eyes of all men and magnified the fame of his exploits from one end of the creation to the other, and granted him besides that thing which his soul earnestly desired. For many times he asked and besought his Lord in prayer, saying thus: "O Lord God of Hosts, let not thy servant come to stand in need of mortal help, and let me not descend from this place, and men see me on the ground. But upon this stone, on which I have stood at thy command and at thy word, grant me to finish the days of my life. Then from it take the soul of thy worshipper, according to the will of thy Lordship."

But perhaps there is someone who says, "What need did he have, or was this required, that he should stand upon a pillar? For on the ground or in that corner could he not please our Lord?" We all know, indeed, and are aware of the fact that God is everywhere, in Heaven and on earth, in the height and in the depth, in the sea and in the abyss, and underneath the earth and above the heavens. And there is no place devoid of his divinity, except men who do not his will. Wherever a man calls upon him in truth, there he finds him. For Jonah called upon him in the lowest abysses, and he heard his prayer and accepted his petition, and from the inside of Sheol below he drew him forth. Again, Daniel cried unto him from the den, and the companions of Hananiah from the fiery furnace, and he sent an angel with his grace according to his petition and was a deliverer and a savior to them. By each one of his servants, wherever they sought him, there he was found: Elijah on Carmel, Abraham on the top of the mountain, quickly he heard their prayer and granted their wish and answered their petition and exalted them.

In the manner that seemed best to his Lordship, in the case of each one of his servants in due season, as was pleasing and good in his eyes, he sent him to preach and to teach. And again, according as he willed, he gave them laws and commandments; the sons of Adam, that they should not eat of the tree; the sons of Seth, that with the daughters of Cain they should not mingle; Noah, the rainbow and the inviolable covenant; Abraham, the sign and seal of circumcision; Moses, the Sabbath and the keeping of the law. Elijah he clothed with zeal, like flaming fire. Isaiah he commanded that he should walk before him naked and barefoot. Jeremiah he commanded to put a yoke and thongs on his neck. To Ezekiel he said,[40] "Shave thy head and beard with a razor, take thy stuff upon thy shoulder and dig through the wall and go out as though insane." Hosea, the holy prophet, he commanded, "Take a wife, a harlot." And to each one of his servants in his own season he commanded to live according to his will; because he has authority as Lord in his creation and as God over the work of his hands, and there is none who can find fault with the free will of his Lordship.

Everyone who hears and observes and does, is kept and exalted and prospered. For Abraham was counted worthy to be called the friend of God, and Moses too was glorified and made chief and leader, while great exploits and wonderful our Lord performed through him. Elijah, too, was taken up and did not taste death. Thus, in the case of Saint Simeon, too: it pleased his Lord to have him stand on a pillar in these days and last times, because he saw the creation as though it were asleep, that by the distress of his servant he might arouse the world from the heaviness of its lethargy of sleep, and that the name of his divinity might be praised through the instrumentality of his believer.

That thou mayest know that truly this was from God, I will tell thee the thing as it was and as it happened. Saint Simeon had a window in the mandra, before which a stone was placed which was three cubits high, and incense and a censer were put upon it. Once during the confinement of the forty days, when about three weeks had passed, there appeared to Saint Simeon a certain goodly man whose face was radiant as the light, who was girded as one who goes to war; and he saw him come and pray before the window of the sacred treasury, After the prayer was ended he went up and stood upon the stone, and, folding his hands behind him, he bowed and raised himself up; then looking at the Saint, again he lifted his hands towards Heaven and gazed upward. Three nights, then, he did thus from dusk to dawn. Thereupon the Saint perceived and understood that for his sake he did thus, and had been sent from the Lord to show him and teach him that thus he should be assiduous in his prayer. And when he ceased after three days and had passed out of sight, the Saint himself went and stood upon it three months. After that, he began to make for himself those small pillars, until he made the one twenty cubits high.

And that thou mayest know that in very truth this thing was from the Lord, that he stood upon a pillar, again I will tell thee that which really was. After he had stood upon those small ones seven years, up to that one twenty cubits high, he had the feeling that he should exchange the twenty cubit one and make one of thirty cubits. So when the Lenten fast drew near, he called that disciple of his who was with him, the one who served him many years, who closed his eyes, and on whose shoulder he laid his head as he surrendered his spirit to his Lord. And he commanded him and said to him, "Before the time when our Lord wills and the door of the mandra is opened, make and set up for me a pillar of two sections, which shall be thirty cubits high." He also summoned workmen and commanded them and said to them, "Before the door is opened, let it be made and erected and placed by the door."

When the door of the mandra was closed, the workmen went about it to hew it. But it was as though something were opposing them, for whenever they quarried out a section and struck it, something smote it and shattered it. So they were hewing and the stones were getting broken, until four weeks had passed, and only two weeks remained before the door would be opened. Then that disciple was troubled and the workmen as well, because the forty days were almost gone, and up to this time they had not accomplished anything. So the disciple came to him by night and called and said to the Saint, in distress, "My Lord, I beseech thy holiness, entreat thy Lord on behalf of this matter, that if it is according to His will, He will remove the difficulty and reveal to thy holiness that thus Satan is opposing us. And if it is not His will, why should we labor in vain, we and the workmen, and not accomplish anything?"

But the Saint refused even to talk with the disciple, and said to him, "Go away, and come tomorrow." He did as he commanded him.

And the next night he came and called and said to him, "My Lord, what does thy holiness command me? Shall we work or stop?" Then the Saint talked with him and encouraged him and said to him, "Be not troubled, for lo! God has corrected it according to his pleasure; and he revealed and made known to me, the sinner, the thing which I sought from him. For there came to me this night a certain man of goodly and pleasant appearance, who said to me, 'Be not discouraged about the matter which thy disciple reported to thee. For thus thy Lord wills, that thou shouldest make for thyself a pillar forty cubits high, and construct it of three sections symbolical of the Trinity, as thou believest.' And he gave me three gifts, pure and white, very beautiful and lovely. And thee also he called by thy name: 'Sacristan So-and-So, take this gift and cry aloud and proclaim and say, "Sing unto the Lord a new song, all the earth."' But now go and do just as I said to thee; and I trust the Lord God that he will open up the door before thee."

And when that disciple arose in the morning and took the workmen with him, that they should go out and look for a suitable stone to hew out those three sections, the Lord opened the door before them, and they found inside the mandra a suitable stone, over which they had been going out and coming in daily. They set to work at it, and by the help of the Lord in one week they quarried and shaped it and prepared it for a pillar and brought it in and placed it at the door of the mandra. So when the Saint opened the door, they brought it in, raised it, and put the pillar in place. And he went up and stood upon it thirty years as a single day.

CHAPTER XXVI

THE DEATH OF MAR SIMEON

And his Lord granted to him that upon it he ended his days, as he requested from God, with great renown, with deeds of beneficence, acts of righteousness, and practices of perfection. And he was of profit to many, and to himself, and the name of his Lord was praised because of him and on his behalf from one end of the creation to the other. And he waxed influential and increased in his honor and exploits in his decease more than in his life-time. The holy church was exalted by him, the horn of Christianity lifted up, and his end was much greater than his beginning, so that if there was any one of divided opinion, his mind was established and he was confirmed in the faith.

For not as an ordinary man did his Lord give him exit from the world, neither did he hide from him the day of his coronation. He revealed it to him in the manner I will describe. After he had been in the mandra seven years, two men appeared to him standing before him in fair and beautiful clothing. One of them grasped in his right hand a measuring rod with which he measured off forty rods, then turned to his companion and said to him, "Whenever this number forty is completed, the measure will be finished, and he will be taken. But I will make a sign the like of which has not been in these times, and then I will take him." And without the Saint fully understanding him, he repeated the measuring twice, speaking in the same way. To the Saint himself about this thing he did not say anything; only they talked with each other not a little while, then disappeared. But he was sure that it was said about him, and he was always very heedful of it. And when he saw that the number drew near, he was looking for that sign of which he had said, "I will make it, and then I will take him;" and he was reflecting as to what sort of sign this would be.

When he saw that sign[41] of anger which occurred in the city Antioch and its district, and he saw the whole creation which assembled there, thousands and tens of thousands, a countless throng, and saw the priests leading their flocks and using great diligence and care, with censers and incense and lighted tapers and crosses, and all the people running from every quarter shouting and with tears and bitter groans, and he also saw that the number was completed, he felt disturbed and summoned his first disciple and said to him privately, "As I see the number is completed, and the sign is very solemn, I do not know—has indeed the appointed time arrived, and am I to be taken? But before the day I will say to thee, because thou hast been with me many years and knowest that clothing of any other sort has never touched my flesh, except these skins: Now let God be thy witness if thou allowest clothing of any other kind to touch my limbs!"

Thus it was that clothing of any other kind did not touch the flesh of the Saint, besides those skins. And his Lord made his departure such as I think none of those born of women in these times had. For there was an assembly of the people and of all humanity, innumerable and of untold size, for fifty-one days after that last sign which occurred in the district, and no one dared either to enter his house, except in fear, or to go out to the field, except in terror. No one was doing any work at all, but upon everyone a stupor had fallen, and they had all given up in despair, and the mind of every one was confused and distracted. They stood looking to see what the Saint would command them; for as though from the mouth of his Lord they looked to receive the command of his Holiness.

After fifty-one days had passed, as we said, there was also that great commemoration in the month Tammuz. After this the Saint never made another commemoration such as that one, whose congregation no one could describe. For since time began there has not been its like in creation. For God had aroused the whole world that he might bring it to the greeting and reverence of his loved one, and might show him his honor while he lived, as he did to Moses the holy when he took him up to the mountain and showed him the promised land, and then took him away. The blessed

Saint Simeon summoned everyone, the priests and their disciples, the nobles and the humble, and exhorted them and comforted them, and gave them commands and admonitions that they should keep the laws and precepts of our Lord. Like a father good and compassionate, who commanded his beloved children, he said to them, "Go in the peace of our Lord Jesus Christ, and keep vigil in your districts three days. Then go out in the name of our Lord and set to work, and let every one do his task. And I trust the Lord God, that he will be your preserver."

And after he had dismissed every one to his work in peace, thirty days passed, when, on the twenty-ninth day of the month Ab[42] at the eleventh hour of the night between Saturday and Sunday, he suddenly felt ill, as some disciples were present with him; and pain struck him, and he began to suffer, and his whole body was feverish. He felt ill all day Sunday and Monday and Tuesday. Then loving kindness was shown him by God, which on account of its magnitude is perhaps difficult to believe; but to believers everything is credible, to those who know that to their Lord everything is possible. The sign was this: the heat was severe and so intense that the ground was burned from its glow, in those days during the going out of Ab and the beginning of Elul.[43] And to the Saint this loving kindness was shown which I will describe; and perhaps for this purpose also that intense heat came to pass, for the sake of a test, and by reason of the sign his Lord ordained to give him an earnest of the reward of his labor, while he was in this world. For the wind blew softly, and it was cool and balmy as though heavenly dew were dropping upon the Saint. And pleasant fragrance exhaled and came from it, the like of which has not been told in the world. There was not one odor of it, but wave on wave came whose several odors were different from one another, so that neither spices nor sweet herbs and pleasant smells which are in the world, can be compared to the fragrance of those waves; because it was by the care and providence of God. For neither were they exhaled in every place, nor even the whole length of that staircase, but from its middle and upward wave on wave went forth, nor in the whole mandra. No one perceived it, because of the incense which was ascending.

And when that first disciple saw it, who loved him and stayed with him day and night and did not go away from him, especially in those days when he was ill, he comforted him and encouraged him and said to him, "Behold, my lord, how thy Lord loves thee. For lo, He has done thy will and pleasure in everything, and brought all the world to greet thee and honor thee; and lo, He shows thee thy honor in thine eyes. And this, too, which has not been the lot of man, He has done in the case of thy Holiness; and even now He has given thee the earnest of the reward of thy labors, for it was never heard nor spoken of in the world that incense exhaled in this manner; from this time thy Lord honors thee as thy labors deserve. But we beseech by thy God whom thou hast loved from thy youth, fill thy holy mouth with blessing and bless thy disciples, because thy perfection knoweth how we honor and worship thy righteousness." So he blessed them, and admonished and commanded them that they should tell no one about this incense. For the Saint himself knew that in very deed it was a divine providence.

On the fourth day of the week, in the second of the month Elul, at the ninth hour, as all his disciples were present with him, he gave command to those two about their companions and committed them all to our Lord. Then he stood up erect, and three times bowed, and again raised himself up, and gazed heavenward, and turned about and looked on all the world. Then all the people who were there cried out, "Bless us, Master." Again he gazed eastward and westward and on every side, then raised his hand from the inside of his cloak and blessed them, thrice committing them to our Lord. As his disciples stood and kept hold of him, as sons a father good and kind, again they said to him, "Master, bless thy servants, we beseech by thy Lord, who has done thy will and is taking thee to himself as thou didst ask him."

Thereupon he grasped the hands of both of them and commanded them about one another, that they love one another. He commanded them also about their companions. Then raising his hands to Heaven he committed them to our Lord. Then again he lifted his eyes to Heaven and smote three times upon his heart with his right hand, and bowed and put his head on the shoulder of that first disciple. And the two disciples put their hands upon his eyes, and he surrendered his spirit to his Lord. So he fell asleep, and the labor and weariness and pain were over, when he put his head on the shoulder of that disciple, while they put their hands upon his eyes, and all the people stood and looked at him.

CHAPTER XXVII

MOURNING AND EULOGY ON THE OCCASION OF MAR SIMEON'S DEATH

But his disciples, because they feared the people, lest the village should gather and come to snatch him away and there should be bloodshed and murder, made him a coffin and put him in it on the top of the pillar, until they might secure for it a place of honor. Suddenly this was reported, and the rumor went out and spread in all the world. And astonishment and consternation seized everybody, and amazement fell upon all flesh, because so suddenly they heard this which they had not expected. Everybody's mind fell into blank confusion, their brains grew numb and hands feeble, and mourning and grief fell upon many. There were some, indeed, who mourned and sorrowed, and some again who rejoiced and gave thanks. So that rejoicing was mingled with sadness, consolation with mourning, and cheerfulness with gloom. For some wept and were depressed; and others, again, lifted their hands to heaven, and to God Almighty gave thanks and blessings, that this report and the good news of the coronation of Christ's servant had reached their ears. This event was one of sadness and of joy; of mourning and of consolation. For it was sad, that such a wise pilot who steered his worldly ship with divine wisdom was taken away from the world. But it was a matter of rejoicing, that the fleshly ship of the watchful mariner had entered and arrived at the port of bliss, laden with a rich cargo, and he had escaped the billows which continually buffeted him. Ceased now the tempests with winds and hurricanes, which had battled with him and against him. His gain in trade was an abiding possession, and his Lord he gladdened with his profits.

On the other hand, it was an occasion for lamentation, my brethren, because such a wise master-builder, laden with the petition of the weight of the creation, had been taken away from the world. For like beams in an edifice, his prayers held firm the world. On the other hand, it was matter for cheer, because his Master had stretched out the hand of relief and given him strength and endurance. He began in His Name, and finished in His Goodness. His building went up to the finish and was not shaken by the winds and rain and flood of sin, which throughout forty-seven years surged against it with every sort of trial.

Again it was a matter of tears and sorrow, because such a spiritual father, who nourished and brought up his children with heavenly nourishment, had departed from their midst. Again it was a matter of gladness, that even if he did leave his children orphans in the flesh, yet he like a heavenly eagle soared upward in flight and mounted to the craggy eyrie on high, leaving behind all fears and ascending from all harms.

Again, the orphans and widows wept with tears and sighs, saying, "Where shall we seek or where find thee, who sustained and nourished us next to his Lord?" The oppressed remembered and feared, and the downtrodden were disquieted, being depressed and troubled, saying, "Woe to us, because now is opened against us the mouth of ravening and voracious wolves. And whom shall we call to awake him, the strong lion, who slumbers and lies in the deathsleep, from whose roaring they trembled, and from whose terrible voice they hid themselves like foxes in their holes?" The sufferers, too, bewailing him said, "Whither shall we go, or where seek and find a healer like thee or comparable to thee and similar to thee? Before the disease saw thee, it fled, and before the pain had come to thee it vanished; and at thy word more than by all roots and drugs they were cured."

The church, moreover, wept for him with her children, priests and their parishes, and shepherds and their flocks, with grief and with joy, with tears and with supplications, with sighs and prayers, with sorrow and cheer. For in grief they sought him who was to them as a quiet harbor and peaceful asylum. For whenever sprang up any sort of evil, which is always a trouble and disturbance of the good, either winds of sin or hurricane of false doctrine, he stood ready boldly, like a wise master-builder, and like a skilful workman, and like a practical pilot, and like a watchful mariner, and like a trained athlete, and like an instructed scribe, and like an armed warrior clad with the breastplate of righteousness and nerved mightily with the true faith and strengthened spiritually with trust in his Lord. He soared in prayer, and fled for refuge with courage; he raised his eyes to heaven and lifted up his gaze on high, and asked mercy from his Lord, and sought grace and help from his God. He rebuked the winds of sin and they slept, and the whirlwinds of deceit and they became still.

For he roared like a lion, and was a smiter of all who stand on the wrong side. They were comforted then and rejoiced, and their gladness was mingled with thanksgiving and blessing. For they rejoiced and blessed God their Lord, who had given to his servant so that he battled and conquered, fought and won, asked and received, sought and found, and knocked and it was opened to him. He began in truth and finished in righteousness. The horn of the holy church was exalted, and all her sons rejoiced with their priests, and their folds with their flocks. All the teachers of false doctrines were ashamed and confounded, who saw one thing instead of another. They were in distress then, and troubled lest at any time a root of evil should produce a plant of bitterness like unto it, and with the taste of its bitterness should harm and injure many. Then where should we find a healer or a burden-bearer like him or equal to him, who before the ulcer appeared cured it, or before the disease or affliction came, healed it by his prayers?

For there was once a tempest of sin and a storm of evil against the Church of Christ, through a certain evil and wicked man, whose name was Asclepiades, an uncle of the empress. He was chief procurator in the days of Theodosius the emperor; and in the days of John, Bishop of Antioch. The mind of this evil man consented with that of heathen and Jews; but he hated the Christians. He sent out an edict that their synagogues and meeting houses which the Christians had taken from the Jews should be returned to them, and that the Christians should build and purchase some for themselves. And the edict of the king and command of the prefect in regard to this was promulgated in many cities and was read to everyone. Then there was great grief and disappointment among all the Christians, especially because they saw the Jews and heathen clothed in white and appearing glad and merry. But they did not know nor understand, the fools, that quickly sadness and regret would overtake them, and it would be in their case as it was in the days of our Lord, when their fathers and priests lost their money but did not bury the truth. So also now again it happened to them, that the great amount of money they had given they lost, and they became a laughing-stock in the world, while their Sabbaths and synagogues remained deserted in their desolation.

For there came to the blessed Saint Simeon bishops grieved and sorrowing, who told him this; also copies of the letters of the king and prefect they brought with them. And when they read them before the Saint, he was grieved and burned with zeal for his Lord like a flaming fire. And he took a courageous stand and boldly wrote words of might filled with rebuke. He did not call Theodosius "Emperor," but he wrote to him thus: "Since thy heart is exalted and thou hast forgotten the Lord thy God who gave thee the diadem of honor and a royal throne, and thou hast become friend and confederate and abettor of unbelieving Jews, God's just judgment will suddenly overtake thee and all those who are consenting to this business. Then thou wilt lift up thy hands to heaven and say in thy distress, 'In truth, this wrath has come upon me because I played false to the Lord God.'"

When the Emperor read it, his heart trembled and feared, and he was seized with compunction even unto death. He at once commanded, and letters were written to all the cities, that the former letters be annulled, and the Christians and priests of God should be honored. He also dismissed the prefect from his office in deep disgrace. And he wrote letters to the Saint by the hand of princes, in conciliating terms, and asked him to pray for him and bless him and be reconciled to him. So the distress passed away, and there was joy to the church and all its adherents, and the evil one was ashamed with his servants. Thus truth was victorious and God was glorified through his believer.[44]

On account of these and many more things than these they were in grief and sorrow, because had departed from them the blessed father, to whom all the priests of God were like sons; and as a mother her sons, he had cherished them under the wings of his prayers. But they rejoiced and were glad because they saw that the athlete was garlanded, and that the spiritual warrior, who had stood manfully in the contest and fought bravely, had conquered his enemy and was written down on the side of the conquerors; the diligent husbandman, whose seed brought forth a hundredfold; the wise master-builder, whose building was finished and was not shaken by the violence of the winds and the fury of the tempests and the rush of rivers, all the long time they beat upon it; the skillful sailor, whose ship arrived at the port of bliss and was not injured by the many surging billows and the fiercely raging storms which pounded and beat against it through a stretch of years; it opposed them all, and trampled upon their necks by the great help which was from its Lord, and rejoiced its mariner by the multitude of its gains; the faithful steward, who controlled his fellows in righteousness, and received the promise from his Lord, that he should be appointed over his treasury; the practiced scribe, who wrought and taught, and his teaching and the word of his tongue was acceptable, and they meditated on it night and day, men and women, old and young, young men and maidens.

All regions rejoiced in the teaching of the just man,

evil was ashamed, and God was glorified in his good and faithful servant, whose talent was doubled, and his Lord rejoiced over his gain in trade. The horn of the Holy Church was exalted in the end of his labor and in the completion of his struggle. Her mouth was opened in praise and in songs of the spirit; she began to say, rejoicing, while her face was glad and her heart exulted, and her soul was joyful, "Now is exalted my head above mine enemies about me." For she saw with all her sons what honor our Lord bestowed upon her lover, the one who had honored her priests and upheld her laws; and she forgot the shame and pain which had always tormented her. So she lifted up her voice in praise and began to say, "Now, Lord, I will praise thee, for thou answeredst me and becamest to me a Savior."

For not in a simple way did his Lord make the departure for his faithful one, but above all men who lived in his day and generation he magnified his triumphs in his life and death. For while he lived there came from the ends of the earth far distant peoples and barbarian tongues to greet him, to see his radiant and dear face, and to hear his divine teachings, and emperors did him homage in their letters continually by their ambassadors. And again at his death priests came, and so did their parishes and flocks, and the emperor's commander-in-chief with a multitude of soldiers who were under his command. For there was at the time of the Saint's death a generalissimo who held the control of all the East, Ardabur the general, son of Aspar; who were (both) honored like kings in their own dominions. He came bringing with him twenty-one prefects and many tribunes, and an innumerable host of soldiers, and they attended the funeral of the Saint. For the citizens of Antioch entreated the general and besought him with tears and many sighs, that they might bring the Saint in thither, that he might be a defense to their city, which was ruined because of their sins;

that they might be sheltered by his prayers. This was done of the Lord, that he might show how great honor he was bestowing upon him who had loved him and honored him by good work and deeds of righteousness. For he brought him down with very great honor, and in much pomp, priests and chief priests bearing him on their hands, and all the sons of the Holy Church, until they came to the village of Shīḥ, which was about three miles distant from the mandra. And from there, again, he was placed upon a chariot, with generals and chiefs of the cities, and many soldiers surrounding him, and people innumerable and countless. For the villagers came forth for the celebration men and women, old and young, youths and maidens, bond and free, to show their respect for him and receive blessing from him, as they burned incense and carried lighted candles.

CHAPTER XXVIII
FUNERAL AND BURIAL OF MAR SIMEON

The Saint's body was conducted in pomp for five days; for on the second day of the week it went out from the mandra and on Friday entered the great city of Antioch in great pomp and with such chanting as is beyond description, while they burned incense and lighted candles, and sprinkled sweet perfume before it and upon all the people who accompanied it; psalms and spiritual songs were chanted before it, until into the great and holy church—which Constantine the victorious and just Emperor built, whose memory shall be blessed in both worlds—it entered and was placed, a thing which had happened to none of the saints, neither ancient or modern. For no one was ever put in the cathedral church, neither of the prophets nor of the apostles nor of the martyrs, excepting only the blessed Saint Simeon himself. Also the bishop of Antioch himself and all his clergy, every day as a mark of honor chanted hymns of the spirit before him, and served with great silver censers of incense which they placed before him, continually, burning all the time sweet odors and choice incense such as they burned while he was alive, that God might show how greatly he honored him in his life and in his death.

His Lord also showed in his funeral a great triumph through him, such that all the beholders were amazed, and he made known the gift of healing which was given to him from God, such a thing as his labors merited. For there was a man who was possessed of an unclean spirit of an evil demon, who had lived among the tombs many years. The burial place was close to the highway, beside a village whose name was Marwa, and all those who went and came by that road saw him. His speech was taken away, and he was bereft of his reason, and roared all the time as he went to and fro at the door of the burial place. He neither knew anyone, nor did anyone dare to approach him from fear and because of the sound of his roaring.

Now when he saw that the coffin of the Saint's body was passing by upon the chariot, as though mercy from heaven was shown him, and as though for this, too, he had been kept, he left the sepulchre in which he dwelt, and running at full speed, threw himself upon the coffin in which lay the Saint's body. And just as soon as he reached the coffin his demon fled from him and the evil spirit which tormented him left him. His reason returned, he knew and recognized every one, the bond of his tongue was loosed, his mouth opened, and he praised and glorified God; and astonishment seized everyone. So was fulfilled that which is written, "The power which is in his works he shows to his people."[45] And he followed the Saint and entered the city with him. And there he was many days in the church, rejoicing and confessing and glorifying God. Also the victorious and

110

Christian Emperor Leo,[46] worthy of blessed memory, sent letters with ambassadors, with great pains, and wrote to the military commanders and bishops that they should send him the body of the holy Saint Simeon, that he might honor him there in his abode as his works merited, and that their dominion might be guarded through his prayers. Thereupon all Antioch arose with all its inhabitants, and with tears and sighs wrote and entreated of him, "Because our city has no walls, since it fell in the visitation, we have brought him that he may be a wall for us, and we may be protected by his prayers." And with difficulty he was persuaded by them to accede to this request that they should leave him with them. Even to such a degree as this did God magnify his worshipper, and because he honored God he was honored by God and reverenced by men.[47]

So the holy and elect of God, Mar Simeon, was at rest.[48] His struggle was ended, and he received his crown with high renown and with deeds of righteousness, and there was great joy to all who feared God, in the year seven hundred and seventy, at the end of the δωδεκάτη, that is, the twelfth year, and at the beginning of the τρισκαιδεκάτη, that is, the thirteenth year, on the second of the month Elul, on the fourth day of the week. He remained in the mandra, after he was laid at rest in the coffin on the pillar, nineteen days. But in the reckoning of the month it was twenty days, because one day previous must be reckoned to the month for the time of the Saint's death. He was laid at rest on the second of the month, and went out of his mandra on the twenty-first of the month Elul, and entered the city of Antioch on the twenty-fifth of the month, on Friday. For he went out on the second day of the week, and on Friday he entered, that is, after a period of five days, amid rejoicing and in great and magnificent pomp. May his memory be blessed, and his prayers be over the creation forever. Amen!

Here endeth the glorious life of the blessed Mar Simeon.[49]

NOTES

1. *Note to the 2009 edition:* Storax is a semifluid balsam prepared from the inner bark of the oriental sweetgum. It was commonly used in ancient times as incense. (Atchley, p. 6)
2. i.e. Baptism.
3. Assemani's text has: He who had come up from beneath the altar.
4. i.e. the door.
5. This means that he partook of food on the successive Sundays *only*. 9 JAOS 35.
6. Matthew 5:11.
7. *Note to the 2009 edition:* 458 of the Antiochene era = AD 410.
8. *Note to the 2009 edition:* Periodeutes is a clerical rank similar to chorepiscopus. A periodeutes functioned as a traveling presbyter, entrusted with supervising the churches of a given area. See Trombley, *The Chronicle of Pseudo-Joshua Stylites*, p. 63.
9. Nearly ½ pint.
10. Literally, "hot coal". See Isaiah 6.
11. *ḥnāna*, literally "Mercy"; a compound of consecrated earth, oil, and water.
12. *Note to the 2009 edition:* The fourth month of the Babylonian and Hebrew calendars which encompassed the end of June and the beginning of July.
13. Psalms 19:4; cf. Romans 10:18, 1 Thessalonians 1:8.
14. ܡܥܒܪ, read ܡܥܒܪ σελιδιον; Brockelmann, *Lexicon Syr.*, p. 505.
15. A cor = 11 1/9 bushels.
16. i.e., recovered his sight.
17. There is a play on words here in the Syriac.
18. Psalms 147:17.
19. *Note to the 2009 edition:* This passage refers to the emperor Theodosius II and his sisters, Pulcheria, Arcadia, Flaccilla, and Marina, though one or more of these may have been deceased by this time (Bury, *History of the Later Roman Empire*, Vol. 1, p. xvii).
20. MS., Domnīn.
21. Literally, "the image of a mortal king."
22. The reason why the young men wished to escape office was because higher municipal officials were so weighted with heavy expenses that it often ruined their fortunes. Hence they represented the governor's act as a piece of vindictiveness. (Nöldeke, *Sketches from*

Eastern History, p. 217).

23. A kind of large mouse or rat.
24. Read ◦ᵢ◦ᴬ◦ in place of ◦ᵢᴬ◦.
25. Reading ⱱᵒ◦ᴮ in place of ⱱᵢᴮⁱ.
26. The Maronites are probably descendants of these converts who embraced Christianity after Simeon's intercession had, as they believed, freed them from the ravages of wild beasts (Nöldeke, *Sketches from Eastern History*, p. 220).
27. John 14:12.
28. Acts 5:15.
29. Acts 19:12.
30. John 21:25.
31. Literally, "the son of the left hand."
32. Psalms 107:2, 3, 6.
33. "Indian" here means an Ethiopian, as often.
34. Assemani's text has "Amid".
35. The old popular superstition about the demon of the storm and the heavenly deliverer is here crassly transferred to Simeon. (Nöldeke, *Sketches from Eastern History*, p. 222).
36. "House of Wells".
37. A coarse cloak worn by priests.
38. Exodus 19:19.
39. Psalms 37:37.
40. Ezekiel 12:3 ff.
41. In June and September, AD 459, there were severe earthquakes.
42. *Note to the 2009 edition:* The fifth month of the Babylonian and Hebrew calendar which roughly coincides with August.
43. *Note to the 2009 edition:* The sixth month of the Babylonian and Hebrew calendar which roughly coincides with September.
44. On the trustworthiness of this account of Simeon's interference in the matter of the Jewish synagogues, see Nöldeke, *Sketches from Eastern History*, p. 218, and Torrey's article in the present volume, p. 118 ff.
45. Psalms 110:6.
46. Leo the First, who became emperor in the year 457 and died in the year 474. This clause is expunged in Codex Vat. See p. xiv.
47. "Here ends the story of Mar Simeon the Stylite" (Assemani).
48. ["And was crowned the saint Mar Simeon on the second day of the month Elul on the fourth day of the week, at the ninth hour, in the year seven hundred and seventy-one of the Greek Era (i.e. AD 459). Here endeth the excellent story of the course of the life of the perfect saint Mar Simeon of the Pillar. May his prayer aid the sinner who wrote it." (B. M. Add. 12174, fol. 48a)].

113

49. [Dr. Lent's translation and investigations were completed in the spring of 1906. Since then has appeared (in Harnack und Schmidt, *Texte und Untersuchungen*, Bd. 32, Heft 4; Leipzig, 1908) a comprehensive work on the life of the Saint by Lietzmann and Hilgenfeld, to which the latter contributes a German translation of the Bedjan text (pp. 80–180). Hilgenfeld also gives a translation of the Letters of Simeon (pp. 188 ff.), of which the Syriac text, with translation and an investigation regarding authenticity etc., was published by Professor Torrey in *The Journal of the American Oriental Society* in 1899. ED.] *Note to the 2009 edition:* See page 115 of the present volume.

THE LETTERS OF
SIMEON THE STYLITE

by Charles C. Torrey

Professor, Andover Theological Seminary, Andover, MA

Originally published in *The Journal of the American Oriental Society*,
Vol. 20 (1899), pp. 253–276.

Saint Simeon of the Pillar has always been one of the
extremely interesting figures in the history of the Oriental
church, as he is certainly one of the most characteristic.
We are fortunate, too, in possessing considerable detailed
information as to his life and work, derived for the most part
from contemporary sources. This information is not always,
nor even generally, trustworthy, to be sure; but the portion
which we can use with confidence is sufficient to give us
a satisfactory idea of the course of his life, while even the
portion which is least reliable as biography has its value for
the church historian. As is well known, our chief sources for
Simeon's biography are, *first*, the old Syriac *Life*, written
in the year 473 AD[1] by Simeon, son of Apollonius, and Bar
Ḥaṭṭār, son of 'Ūdān,[2] and published by S. E. Assemani in
his *Acta Sanctorum Martyrum*, ii. 268 ff., and by Bedjan
in his *Acta Martyrum et Sanctorum*, iv. 507 ff.; and,
second, the account of Simeon given by his contemporary,
Theodoret of Cyrrhus (died 457), in his *Religious History*.
The main facts of his life are these:[3] He was born in Ṣīṣ, a
small town in the neighborhood of Nicopolis, in northern
Syria, probably between the years 385 and 390. When about

sixteen years of age, he entered a monastery near Antioch. Nine or ten years later, he repaired to Telneššē,[4] some fifty miles northeast of Antioch, where he remained, the most renowned ascetic in the East, until his death in the year 459. The last thirty-seven years of his life were spent on the top of pillars of increasing height; the one occupied by him during the last thirty years being more than sixty feet high. After his death, his body was carried with great pomp to Antioch, and buried there; though Constantinople coveted the honor, and the Emperor Leo himself had planned to have the body brought to that city.

Of the few writings attributed to Simeon, only the *Letters* can lay any claim to genuineness. These—some of them very well known and often referred to—are found in different places; and, with a single exception, are concerned with the theological controversies which rent the Eastern church asunder in the middle of the fifth century. Three of these letters, found only in certain ancient manuscripts of the British Museum, have never been published, though attention has often been called to them, e.g., by Wright, *Syriac Literature*, p. 55, and by Nöldeke, *Orientalische Skizzen*, p. 239. It is the principal purpose of this article to edit and examine these three, with especial reference to the question of their genuineness; though as this purpose necessarily involves at least a partial comparison of the other letters, I have thought it best to bring them all together here.

One of the most celebrated of the letters which Simeon is said to have written is the one concerning the Jewish synagogues, addressed to the Emperor Theodosius II (AD 408–450). At the time when Simeon was beginning to be famous, Jews and Christians were in bitter strife; and the latter having the power in their hands, the former were in danger of losing their rights as well as their property. Many synagogues, especially, were either burned, or seized and made to serve as Christian churches; and the efforts of the emperor to secure to the Jews their rights as citizens, and partially to restore the property stolen from them, were very displeasing to many of the warmer partisans of the church. The text of the letter is given in the *Life*. I reproduce it here from Assemani, *Bibliotheca Orientalis*, i. 254, and add the variant readings of Bedjan's manuscript (*Acta Martyrum et Sanctorum*, iv. 637, line 11 ff.).[4]

"Because[5] in the pride of your heart you have forgotten the Lord your God, who gave you the crown of majesty and the royal throne, and have become a friend and comrade and abettor of the unbelieving Jews; know that of a sudden the righteous judgment of God will overtake you and all those who are of one mind with you in this matter. Then you will lift up your hands to heaven, and say in your distress, 'Of a truth because I dealt falsely with the Lord God this punishment has come upon me.'"

The story of this letter,[6] according to the *Life*, was the following. The emperor's prefect, Asclepiodotus[7] by name, issued an order commanding the Christians in this region to restore to the Jews all the synagogues which had been taken from them by violence. This order produced great consternation among the Christians, while the Jews were in high feather. A number of bishops came to Simeon and told him what was being done; whereupon he wrote this letter. The emperor, upon receiving it, revoked the obnoxious edict, dismissed Asclepiodotus from his office, and sent a humble reply to Simeon.

Nöldeke[8] pronounces this version of the matter scarcely credible, and with good reason. Still, there is, perhaps, no sufficient ground for denying the genuineness of the letter. Theodoret, an independent witness, writing some time before Simeon's death, plainly refers to this rebuke of the Emperor Theodosius in his *Religious History*, near the end of his biography of the Stylite. Speaking of Simeon's boldness and zeal for the church, he says νῦν μὲν ἑλληνικῇ δυσσεβείᾳ μαχόμενος, νῦν δὲ τὴν Ἰουδαίων καταλύων θρασύτητα, ἄλλοτε δὲ τὰς τῶν αἱρετικων συμμορίας σκεδαννύς · καὶ ποτὲ μὲν βασιλεῖ περὶ τούτον ἐπιστέλλων, ποτὲ δὲ τοὺς ἄρχοντας εἰς τὸν Θεοῦ ζῆλον ἐγείρων, κτλ.; where the connection of the clause "sending letters to the emperor about these things" with the preceding, "breaking down the presumption of the Jews," is beyond question, in view of the other narrative.[9]

We can hardly doubt, therefore, that some such written communication was sent to Theodosius by the Stylite. Of the letter which we have, this at least may be said, that it is what we should expect a man like Simeon to write under such circumstances. As for the specific occasion, it is true, as Nöldeke points out, that the story told here of the order to restore the synagogues seems to be discredited by the witness of a document which has come down to us from that very controversy; namely, an edict of Theodosius addressed to Asclepiodotus, dated in the year 423, commanding that no more synagogues be seized or destroyed, and *that restitution be made for those of them which have already been consecrated to Christian use*;[10] the implication being that such could no longer be given back to their former owners. But there is abundant evidence that the emperor and his officers had no small difficulty with this matter of the synagogues, and that it had been the subject of lively dispute. See the *Codex Theodosianus*, xvi. 8, 9. 12. 20. 21; and notice that in this same year 423, between February and June, three successive edicts relating to the matter were promulgated (*ibid.*, 25, 26. 27). It is not unlikely that the monks and the local civil authorities were on opposite sides here (as, for example, Graetz, *Geschicte der Juden*, vol. iv. p. 455, takes for granted); and it may be that what called out Simeon's letter was some proceeding on the part of Syrian officials based on the former less definite laws.

In that case, the emperor's order to Asclepiodotus, referred to above, might well have been hailed by the monks as a victory for their party. Or, again, it is quite possible that when synagogues were seized after the promulgation of this edict of 423, and in violation of it, the attempt was made to punish the offenders by making them restore the buildings and pay damages, as narrated in our history. Of course the part played by Simeon in this matter was far less important than the popular report made it. The emperor's new edict was called forth by the same disturbances which stirred up the monk to write his letter; and it is not at all likely that the prefect Asclepiodotus was dismissed in the way narrated by Simeon's biographers.

It is intrinsically probable that at this time and in this part of the world a letter to the emperor dictated[11] by such a well known saint as Simeon already was (even if we date the letter as early as 422 or 423) would have been copied and preserved long enough to have been used by biographers who wrote only a short time after his death. There is nothing, therefore, to decide against the supposition that we have before us the letter actually sent in Simeon's name to Theodosius; though the character of the source in which it stands, and our knowledge of the freedom with which even the best of early historians invented such documents to adorn their narrative, make skepticism justifiable.

The remaining letters ascribed to the Stylite are all concerned with the theological controversies of the fifth century.

The best known among these is the letter approving the council of Chalcedon, quoted in part by Evagrius (*Eccl. Hist.*, p. 58), and afterward cited by other historians. The circumstances under which it was written are narrated as follows by Evagrius.

The emperor Leo (I.) Thrax (reigned 457–474) sent out, soon after his accession to the throne, a circular letter[12] to the bishops of the empire and to a few of the most celebrated monks, requesting their judgment upon the Council of Chalcedon. Simeon Stylites, who was the most noted of the monks addressed,[13] wrote to the emperor in reply, approving the council; and at the same time sent a letter of similar tenor to Basil, bishop of Antioch, who, it seems, had also written to ask for his judgment, perhaps with the added purpose of influencing him to send a favorable reply to the emperor. This letter to Basil is the one quoted by Evagrius, who hints that he had also at his disposal the letter of Simeon to Leo, and would have included it in his history if it had not been too long. The letter ran thus (in the translation of the *Bohn Library*):

> "To my lord, the most religious and holy servant of God, the archbishop Basil, the sinful and humble Simeon wishes health in the Lord. Well may we now say, my lord, Blessed be God, who has not rejected our prayer, nor withdrawn his mercy from us sinners. For, on the receipt of the letters of your worthiness, I admired the zeal and piety of our sovereign, beloved of God, which he manifested and still manifests towards the holy fathers and their unshaken faith. And this gift is not from ourselves, as says the holy apostle, but from God, who through your prayers bestowed on him this readiness of mind." . . . . "On this

account I also, though mean and worthless, the refuse of the monks, have conveyed to his majesty my judgment respecting the creed of the 630 holy fathers assembled at Chalcedon, firmly resolving to abide by the faith there revealed by the Holy Spirit; for if, in the midst of two or three who are gathered together in his name, the Savior is present, how could it be otherwise than that the Holy Spirit should be throughout in the midst of so many and so distinguished holy fathers?" . . . . "Wherefore be stout and courageous in the cause of true piety, as was also Joshua the son of Nun, the servant of the Lord, in behalf of the Children of Israel. I beg you to salute from me all the reverend clergy who are under your holiness, and the blessed and most faithful laity."

The evidence for the genuineness of this letter is in general much like that appealed to in the case of the preceding, but is considerably stronger. Evagrius has an excellent reputation for trustworthiness as a historian, and wrote in Antioch, where a letter dictated by this saint at the pinnacle of his fame (not more than two years before his death) would certainly have been preserved. There seems to be no reason to doubt that Leo wrote to Simeon on this occasion, as attested by Evagrius, the *Codex Encyclius*,[14] and many subsequent historians, and denied by none. And the testimony is uniform that all of those addressed by the emperor returned answers favorable to the Council of Chalcedon, excepting only Timotheus of Alexandria and Amphilochius of Side. Note especially the testimony of the Monophysite historian Zacharias of Mytilene (Land, *Anecdota Syriaca*, vol. iii. p. 142). The letter to Basil of Antioch has, therefore, strong indirect support; and it is yet more deserving of confidence because of its contents. It is a very uninteresting production, made up largely of commonplace phrases, which are drawn out at considerable length. The only plausible reason for inventing such a letter would have been the purpose to show that Simeon approved the Council of Chalcedon; but it is sufficiently obvious that this colorless, almost indifferent utterance could never have been forged as a Chalcedonian party document.

There is another letter, said to have been written by Simeon at about this time, in which his adherence to the 'emperor's party' is attested. This is the letter from Simeon to Eudocia, the widow of Theodosius II., quoted by Cyril of Scythopolis (middle of the sixth century), in his *Vita Euthymii* (Cotelerius, *Ecclesiae Graecae Monumenta*, tom. ii. p. 271), and by Nicephorus Callistus, *Eccl. Hist.*, xv. 13. The latter tells the story as follows.

The empress Pulcheria, having become reconciled to her beautiful sister-in-law (now removed to a safe distance), wished to see her become orthodox, and employed every possible influence to this end. Eudocia, half persuaded by the letters and entreaties she received, finally wrote to Simeon Stylites, asking his guidance and promising to follow it. The letter was sent by the chorepiscopus Anastasius. Simeon replied:

"Know, my child, that the devil, seeing the wealth of your virtues, sought to sift you as wheat; moreover, that corrupter Theodosius, having become the receptacle and instrument of the evil one,[15] both darkened and disturbed your God-beloved soul. But be of good courage, for your faith has not left you. I wonder, however, exceedingly at this, that having the fountain close at hand you do not recognize it, but hasten to draw the water from afar. You have near by the inspired Euthymius; follow his counsels and admonitions, and it will be well with you."[16]

Eudocia followed this advice, and was directed by Euthymius to hold to the doctrine of the four councils of Nicaea, Constantinople, Ephesus (431); and Chalcedon.

Regarding this letter there is little to be said. It may well be genuine, though there is, of course, room for doubt. Even if it is a forgery for the glory of Euthymius, as is possible, it shows, at least, what views the Stylite was commonly believed to hold.[17]

But the question as to Simeon's theological position during the last years of his life—that is, at the time when the above-mentioned letters to Leo, Basil, and Eudocia, are supposed to have been written—is raised anew by the three hitherto unpublished letters of which mention has already been made. All three are decidedly controversial, and in them the Stylite speaks as a bitter opponent of the Chalcedonense.

The letters are found in two ancient Syriac manuscripts of the British Museum. One of these, Add. 12154 (no. DCCCLX. in Wright's *Catalogue*), dated by Wright at the end of the 8th or beginning of the 9th century, is a manuscript of miscellaneous contents, of which the first section is a collection of Monophysite party documents (fol. 1–18). The thirty-third section contains the three letters (*Catalogue*, vol. ii., p. 986), extending from fol. 199*b* to fol. 201*a*. The first of them is addressed to the Emperor Leo (I.); the second, to the abbot Jacob of Kaphrā Reḥīmā; the third, to John, bishop of Antioch (died 442).

The second manuscript, Add. 12155 (no. DCCCLVII. in the *Catalogue*), is a large and beautifully written codex of the 8th century. It is a Monophysite compilation; and contains as its twenty-ninth section (fol. 229a; *Catalogue*, vol. ii. p. 951) the first of the three letters just mentioned, namely the one addressed to the Emperor Leo. There is prefixed to it a superscription occupying several lines; otherwise, the text corresponds closely to that of the other manuscript.

I give here the text of Add. 12154 (A), adding in the case of the letter to Leo the variant readings of Add. 12155 (B).[18]

The Letters of the Holy Mar Simeon the Stylite, which testify concerning him that he did not accept the Council of Chalcedon.

First Letter: To the Emperor Leo, who reigned after Marcian. When I received the letters[19] of your Royal Highness, I at first expected to rejoice with great joy; because I hoped for the rectifying and annulling of those things which were done not long ago in the accursed Council of Chalcedon, so impudently and wickedly, contrary to the word of truth; when the church of God was disturbed by the innovation and false teaching of accursed and perverse heretics. But when some time elapsed, and that which I was hoping for did not come to pass, pains even more grievous than the former came upon my feeble old age, as I saw what things these are, which are perpetrated and done amongst the leaders of the church. But I believe him who said, "In the latter days I will pour out my spirit upon all flesh, and they shall know me, from the least of them to the greatest; and no one shall say to his fellow, 'Know the Lord.'"

To this hope, therefore, I hold fast, as to an anchor, guarding and keeping it unto the end; and all the world cannot move me from it. And I in my weakness beseech your Royal Highness, for the faith of those holy fathers who met at Nicaea, that you preserve it spotless and unimpaired for the holy church of God unto the end.[20]

Second Letter: To Mar Jacob of Kaphrā Reḥīmā.[21]

To our Spiritual Brother in Christ; adorned with graces illustrious and divine; zealous for the orthodox faith of the fathers, which we have learned from prophets, apostles, and saints; the Archimandrite, Mar Jacob of Kaphrā Reḥīmā; from the mean and weak sinner, Simeon, who stands upon the pillar near the village Telnešī; great and exceeding peace in the Lord.

First of all, I beseech you to offer prayers to God for me, that He may give me strength and patience, on this stone upon which I stand; and I also make supplication to God for my sins.

As for the rest: Since your Reverence has sent to me by Mar Thomas, your pupil, requesting that the anathema which I once uttered upon the Council of Chalcedon be put in writing by me and sent to your Reverence; to be used for the consolation and confirmation of the orthodox everywhere, and for the stopping of the mouth of perverse heretics: This I say to you, my Beloved; that I have hope and confidence in God, whom I serve and worship; and I confess Him and believe in Him, whose truth you and I will keep unto the end. I have not approved, and will not approve, that council of perverse heretics which was convened at Chalcedon; nor the evil which was perpetrated by it, and the sinful and wicked deed which they did to the holy martyr Dioscurus.[22]

But I have cursed, and will curse, that wicked council which was convened at Chalcedon; and every one who has approved or shall approve it, or who has been, or shall be, like minded with those who composed it; unless he has repented or shall repent. Moreover, a writing, signed by these calumniators,[23] bears witness for me that I did not approve them, nor did I write anything to that effect; nor can they prove that I ever gave them countenance in any way; nor will any one assert that I did, unless he wishes to destroy his soul by lying and slander. For verily I, the weak and sinful, am a partner with all those holy and saintly fathers, three hundred and eighteen in number, who assembled at Nicaea; and with the hundred and fifty who met at Constantinople; and with the two hundred and twenty who assembled together with the holy Cyril at Ephesus, and cursed and cast out the wicked Nestorius. Moreover, I have been and am a partner with the holy martyr Mar Dioscurus, Patriarch of the metropolis Alexandria; him who was unjustly and wickedly driven into exile, as though he were an evil doer, by perverse heretics, enemies of the truth; those who are like minded with the wicked Nestorius, and with Leo of Rome, and with the unrighteous Emperor Marcian.

As I have already said, the truth which I have learned from apostles and from holy fathers and saints, in this I abide unto the very end of my life; nor will I basely deny that work of grace which was wrought through the coming of God our Savior in human nature; who came down and was incarnated of the Holy Spirit and the Virgin Mary, and was born of her in her virginity, and endured all that came upon him in order that he might redeem the life of all mankind.

If then, my Lord, there is any one who is of doubting mind, let him be confirmed in the faith of the holy fathers, and in these things which we have written. And do you be in good health, and rejoicing in spirit and body. Pray for me that I may be one of God's elect.

Third Letter, also written by Simeon himself: To John of Antioch, concerning Nestorius.

To the holy and God-loving Mar John, Bishop of Antioch, from Simeon the feeble in the Lord, greeting.

Having heard, my Lord, from faithful men that you have been summoned by the most pious emperor to attend the holy council, for which, on account of Nestorius and his blasphemies, he is striving to assemble the holy bishops at Ephesus; and that your Holiness, as is reported, does not wish to join their assembly: I in my insignificance urge your Holiness, not to delay to go up to the holy council of Ephesus, and to become an ally of our holy father Cyril, and a participant in the holy synod which is with him, in cursing the misguided Nestorius—if so be that he come not to repentance.

If this shall not be done by you, I know well that there will be no peace in the churches of the East; but that, on the contrary, great disturbances will arise. Nay, surely it is for you to do this, which will please God, rejoice the king, and establish peace in the churches of the East.

As was remarked above, the manuscript Add. 12155, which contains only the letter to the Emperor Leo, prefixes to it a superscription several lines in length. This superscription, which is rubricated, reads as follows:[24]

"The Letter which Mar Simeon the Stylite wrote to the Emperor Leo, who reigned after Marcian; which was called forth by the conduct of Theodoret of Cyrrhus, the heretic; who approached the blessed Mar Simeon, hoping to lead him astray with the heresy of the Diophysites, and sowed words of blasphemy in the ears of the blessed Mar Simeon. Wherefore he clothed himself with zeal for the faith, and wrote this letter to the Emperor Leo, in distress and anguish of spirit."

In this superscription, the fact appears once more which has been sufficiently evident throughout these Syriac documents; namely, that whether Simeon Stylites wrote the three letters or not, they are the work of a vehement partisan, and were circulated to serve as Monophysite party weapons. The general superscription found in manuscript A, for example ("Letters of Simeon, which testify that he did not accept the Council of Chalcedon"), plainly implies the existence of a more or less widespread belief (held and proclaimed by "impudent and wicked heretics") that Simeon *did* accept the Council of Chalcedon. We know, in fact, that this saint, whose dictum was of such great importance, was claimed not only by Monophysites and Chalcedonians, but also by Nestorians. In at least one of the three letters, moreover, the writer's main purpose is, professedly, to silence his calumniators. The letter addressed to the abbot Jacob of Kaphrā Reḥīmā was intended (to use its own words) "to be used for the consolation and confirmation of the orthodox everywhere, and for the stopping of the mouth of perverse heretics." And a little further on, the writer implies that his Chalcedonian enemies have produced documents (which he brands as forgeries) in support of their assertion. "I did not approve [the council]," he says, *"nor did I write anything to that effect,* nor can they prove that I ever gave them countenance in any way; nor will any one assert that I did, unless he wishes to destroy his soul by lying and slander."

That is, it is not a question of Simeon's conversion from Melkite to Monophysite views; he says here (or is made to say) most distinctly that he never at any time gave the hated 'synod' his support. If, then, this letter to Jacob is genuine, it follows that the letters above quoted or alluded to, preserved by Evagrius, Cyrillus Scythopolitanus, and the rest, are all forgeries.

But can Simeon have been the author of these Monophysite epistles? From all that we know of his surroundings and the influences to which he was subjected, we should expect to find him a Chalcedonian. He had passed all his life in the Antiochian district; a district in which sectional pride had been strong during the last decades of his life, while the 'Antiochian party' still held its ground and made its influence felt. It is true that as early as the middle of the fifth century the Syrian theology was losing its hold on the laity,[25] and we know that among the monks, especially, the Monophysite doctrines were more and more decidedly gaining the upper hand in this region, as in most other parts of the East. But the great Monophysite triumphs here came after Simeon's day; while he lived, war was waged in Syria quite as bitterly between Nestorians and men who held views like those of Ibas of Edessa, as between Monophysites and their opponents. What is much more important, Simeon was not a mere monk among monks, but was hand in glove with the Syrian leaders. Theodoret, the pillar of the Antiochians, was his friend. We know that Domnus II of Antioch (patriarch, 442–449), a steady opponent of the Monophysites from the first,[26] was received by Simeon with especial favor on at least one occasion. See the story told in the Life (p. 63 of the present volume), and repeated, in somewhat different form, by Evagrius (*Eccl. Hist.*, p. 18). The impression of the Stylite which we gain from the Life and from our other sources is that he was in full sympathy and cooperation with those who were the acknowledged leaders of the Syrian church. The council of Chalcedon reinstated Theodoret and Ibas, who, together with Domnus and others, had been deposed at Ephesus in the council of 449. This action may well have given the bishops and clergy of this region a strong added reason for accepting the Chalcedonense, as in fact they generally did.[27] It is natural to suppose that Simeon was of one mind with them in this.

The evidence afforded by the letters (whether genuine or not) given by Evagrius and the *Vita Euthymii* has already been noticed. Their testimony to Simeon's reputation as a Chalcedonian is weighty; that furnished by the story of Euthymius and the letter to Eudocia deserving, perhaps, especially to be emphasized.[28] And there is another noteworthy bit of evidence of a somewhat similar nature. In the *Edessene Chronicle*, lxix., the death of Simeon Stylites is recorded, as the event distinguishing the year 771 (AD 459).[29] This means, as Hallier remarks, that he is classed as a Chalcedonian. The compiler of the *Chronicle*, who is a Chalcedonian with an added Nestorian bias, writes with such strong party prejudice that he passes over the Monophysite saints and dignitaries in silence (Hallier, *Edess. Chron.*, p. 74 f.).

In view of this array of testimony, direct and indirect, the presumption against the three Monophysite "Letters of Simeon the Stylite" is very strong. The argument from silence, moreover, adds its weight. These letters, if genuine, must have been very widely known. One was addressed to the emperor himself; another to the patriarch of Antioch, about to set out on his ill-fated journey to the first council at Ephesus; the third was expressly intended to be circulated as a campaign document, being the final dogmatic utterance of the great ascetic. But they are never mentioned, either by Monophysite historians or by others; nor does anybody outside of these two Syriac manuscripts seem ever to have heard of them.

In the letters themselves, there are not wanting indications which also tend to show that they are forgeries. With regard to the chronology presupposed in the first letter, this fact is perhaps worthy of notice: Simeon speaks of himself as having waited more than a reasonable time after receiving the emperor's letter (and returning his answer?), in hope that measures would be taken to undo what had been done at Chalcedon. But being disappointed in this hope, he finally wrote the present letter. Now Leo, who came to the throne in February 457, probably sent out his circular letters in the year 458, but possibly even later.[30] In any case, the interval of time before Simeon's death (September 459) would be very short—though perhaps not too short—for such a (second) reply as this from the saint.

In the second letter, the self-description in the address, "Simeon, who stands upon the pillar near the village Telnešī," is suspicious. It would hardly have occurred to the saint to describe himself in just this way, especially as he was the only Simeon Stylites in the world. But at a later day, when there had been other pillar-saints who bore the name Simeon, it would be necessary to mention the locality in order surely to identify the writer of this document.

The third letter is distinctly a *vaticinium ex eventu*.

Whether or not John of Antioch was secretly a friend of Nestorius, and purposely managed to arrive late in Ephesus,[31] it is quite incredible that any one, even in the city of Antioch, could thus have foretold the course which events would take, and the meeting of that "holy synod" which was to be held by Cyril and his monks.[32]

It is, of course, unnecessary to argue that the superscriptions prefixed to the letters in our two manuscripts belong to a later day than that of the Stylite. As for the part played by Theodoret in provoking the epistle to Leo, the death of this friend of Simeon's took place probably before the emperor sent out his circular letter, and certainly before this epistle could have been written.

Finally, most interesting evidence of the forgery is to be found in a fourth Syriac letter belonging to this same group. It is contained in both of the manuscripts, where it immediately follows the "Letter (or letters) of Simeon." I give, as before, the text of Add. 12154 with the variant readings of Add. 12155.[33]

> "The letter which Alexander of Mabbōg and Andreas of Samosata[34] wrote to John of Antioch and Theodoret of Cyrrhus, about the holy Mar Simeon the Stylite and Mar Jacob of Kaphrā Reḥīmā.
>
> To the Holy and Reverend, our spiritual Fathers.
>
> As for the rest: When we received the saintly letters of your God-loving selves, we were filled with great joy, rejoicing especially because of the news of your good health. But those things distress us exceedingly which we learned from your letters concerning the things which Simeon and Jacob wrote to you. But this we urge upon your Holiness, inasmuch as they have dared to write these things contrary to the truth which we hold; that even if you

see them raising the dead to life, you put no faith in them, but count them as the rest of the heretics."

It is at once clear that this curious epistle, sent "from Alexander of Hierapolis and Andreas of Samosata to John of Antioch and Theodoret of Cyrrhus, about Simeon the Stylite and Jacob of Kaphrā Reḥīmā"(!), was written to serve as a voucher for the genuineness of the other three. In particular, it is designed to show that Jacob of Kaphrā Reḥīmā, to whom Simeon's two-edged confession of faith was addressed, had been, as he still continued to be, a strong ally of Simeon's in opposition to these misguided leaders of the Syrian church. A still more important purpose of the document appears when it is brought into connection with the mysterious words of the letter to Jacob, where Simeon is made to say: "Moreover, *a writing, signed by these calumniators*, bears witness for me that I did not approve them." This is the "writing," beyond any question. The whole thing is very well managed. In view of the contents of our epistle number two, which, be it noted, is said to be only the reiteration of former utterances, there could be no doubt as to the nature of the "things which Simeon and Jacob wrote" to John and Theodoret. Thus there is secured the written testimony of four of the foremost anti-Monophysites of this region that Simeon Stylites spurned their doctrines, and was in turn rejected from their fellowship.

We have, then, in these four Syriac letters, an interesting example of that forgery of documents which often played such an important part in the fierce controversies of the fifth and following centuries.[35] The temptation to this misuse of Simeon's name was especially strong; though it was a thing that could not easily be done until after his generation had passed away. He had written no books (if, indeed, he could read and write at all), and therefore a forgery in his name would be the less easily exposed.[36] His support was no small prize to be gained, for he was looked up to as an inspired man, gifted with superhuman knowledge and power. Even the most sober-minded and best educated of those who knew him personally—such as Theodoret, for example—believed him to be a constant worker of miracles. His fame continued unabated after his death;[37] and it is not surprising that some time after, perhaps in the following century, when the bone and sinew of Christian Syria was already Monophysite, and the strife with "Synodites" was still incredibly bitter, some less scrupulous controversialist should have dared to invent these oracles of the great saint.

It is probable that we have the forged documents complete in manuscript A. They seem to be the work of a single writer, and it is hardly likely that the collection ever contained any others. The scribe of the manuscript B (or of one of its ancestors), as is evident, chose to save himself time and trouble by omitting the two longest of the letters; copying only the first, with its secondary superscription, and the fourth.

APPENDIX

A few words regarding the principal manuscripts of the Syriac *Life of Simeon* may not be out of place, in view of the many conflicting statements which are current. The three best known manuscripts are the *Codex Vaticanus clx.*, and two codices of the British Museum, namely Add. 12174, and Add. 14484. The colophon of the Vatican codex reads as follows (I copy the text from Bedjan, *Acta Martyrum et Sanctorum*, iv. p. 648 f.):[38]

> May God and his Christ remember for good Simeon bar Apollon, and Bar Ḥaṭar the son of 'Udan, who assumed the labor of making this book,

"The Glorious Deeds of Mar Simeon the Blessed."
They made it by the toil of their hands and the sweat
of their brows. — — — This book was finished in
the month of Nisan, on the 17th of the month, on
the fourth day of the week, in the year five hundred
and twenty-one, of the Antiochian chronology.
— — — And let everyone who reads it pray for
those who undertook the work and made this book,
that God may give them everlasting forgiveness of
sins. Amen and Amen.

Let everyone who reads and makes, pray for
him who wrote. — — — Farewell in our Lord; and
pray for me.

These words have received various interpretations.
Assemani, who, as is well known, believed the priest
Cosmas, a contemporary of the Stylite, to have been the
author of the *Life*, regarded the date here given ("521 of
the Antiochian reckoning" = 473 AD) as the date of the
transcription of this manuscript; and supposed the two
persons named, Simeon son of Apollonius and Bar Ḥaṭṭār
son of Ūdān, to have been mentioned as those at whose
request, or by whose aid, the biography was written.
Wright, who of course rejected the (groundless) ascription
of the work to Cosmas, agreed with Assemani as to the date
of the manuscript (*Syriac Literature*, 1894, p. 56); but says
of the two Syrians (*l.c.*, note 3): "Assemani is mistaken
....These are merely the persons who paid for the writing of
this portion of Cod. Vat. clx." But on both of these points
Wright, as well as Assemani, is certainly in error. The two
Syrians whose names are given were the authors of the
biography, as Nöldeke (*Orientalische Skizzen*, p. 239, note)
and Bedjan (*op. cit.*, p. xiii.) insist. The verb ܪܚܡ, as the latter
remarks, is frequently used in the sense of "compose" (a

book or other writing).[39] He might have added that the word could hardly bear any other interpretation here, inasmuch as the colophon says, after giving the names of these two, "who took the pains to 'make' this book": "for they 'made' it by the labor of their hands and the sweat of their faces." It follows, that AD 473 was the date of the completion of the original work. The scribe of the Vatican manuscript simply reproduced, as usual, the colophon of an older codex; just when he made his copy, we do not know.[40]

The three manuscripts named present somewhat differing recensions of the work, as is of course to be expected in the case of a popular book of this kind. No serious attempt has as yet been made to determine which of these recensions stands nearest to the original. It is generally taken for granted that the Vatican codex is the oldest, and that its version of the history, which is considerably shorter than either of the others, is to be preferred. So, for example, Nöldeke, *Syrische Grammatik*,[2] p. xiii.: "der Vaticanische Text ist übrigens, wie es scheint, im Ganzen ursprünglicher als der des British Museum." But both of these current opinions deserve to be challenged; and in the case of the latter, it seems possible to prove to the contrary, in one important point at least. Bedjan, who printed the text of the London manuscript Add. 14484, dated by Wright in the sixth century, gives in his preface (p. xii. f.) a list of the numerous passages, some of them of considerable length, which are found in the London manuscript (or manuscripts), but are missing in the Vatican codex. An examination of these passages seems to make it plain that the longer recension, represented by the London codices, is to be preferred to the other. A single illustration will suffice. In Bedjan's text, p. 525 f., where the story of Simeon's first entrance into Telnešsē is told, we have a smooth and consistent account, in the well-known style of this book. But no one can read the

Vatican recension here, comparing it with the other, without seeing at once that it is the result of a mere mutilation of the original. A passage a dozen lines long has been cut out bodily; regarding this fact there is no room for doubt. That is, the Roman codex contains a "clipped" version of the *Life*; in which the scribe has abridged from his original in the favorite way, by leaving out here and there passages of varying length.

It is likely that the oldest of our manuscripts stand at several removes from the original, and certain that the text of each has suffered from accidental corruption—aside from the alterations in matter and order. In view of the age of this biography, and the interest attaching to it, some further comparison of the several recensions might be worth while.

NOTES

1. See Appendix, page 134 of the present volume.
2. Wright (*Syriac Literature*, p. 56, note 3) thought this might be a mistake for Uran (Uranius).
3. See the excellent sketch in Nöldeke's *Orientalische Skizzen*, 1892, pp. 224–239.
4. *Note to the 2009 edition*: The Syriac text in this article has been omitted. It may be found in the original article which is available online via http://www.jstor.org.
5. According to our narrative, Simeon, in his righteous indignation dispensed with the customary introductory formula: "To Theodosius, the Emperor," etc.
6. It is also told by the church historian Evagrius (*Eccl. Hist.*, p. 19), who made use of the *Life*.
7. Called in the *Life* Asclepiades.
8. *Orientalische Skizzen*, p. 232.
9. So Assemani, *Bibl. Orient.*, i. 245,
10. *Codex Theodosianus*, xvi. 8, 25 (ed. Haenel, 1837, col. 1604).
11. As Nöldeke observes (*ibid.*, p. 233), it may be doubted whether Simeon could read and write.
12. See Harnack, *Dogmengeschichte*[3], ii. 377, note 1; and the account given by Zacharias Rhetor (Land, *Anecdota Syriaca*, iii. 138 f.).

13. The others mentioned by name are Baradatus and one Jacob. Of the latter Evagrius merely says that he was a Syrian monk (like the other two); the *Codex Encyclius* calls him "Jacob, a monk of Nisibis" (so also Nicephorus Callistus, *Eccl. Hist.*, xv. 19); while Theophanes Confessor (ed. Classen, i. 173) calls him "Jacob Thaumaturgus." The monk intended is evidently the one lauded by Theodoret in his *Religious History*, chap. 21.

14. In Harduin, *Acta Conciliorum*, vol. ii. (1714), p. 690 ff.

15. This clause seems to be a later improvement. It is not found in the older form of the letter.

16. The *Vita Euthymii*, in which the story is told in much greater detail, gives the letter in almost the same words.

17. It was all the more natural that Simeon should show this courtesy to the Palestinian hermit, because Domnus II of Antioch, who was a friend of Simeon's (see below), had formerly been one of Euthymius' pupils.

18. *Note to the 2009 edition*: The Syriac text and the notes associated with it have been omitted here. See note 4.

19. Evidently referring to Leo's circular letter, mentioned above.

20. The reading of this passage is doubtful. The two manuscripts differ at this point, and neither one presents a fully satisfactory text. The original reading was probably this: "I in my weakness beseech your Royal Highness to keep the faith of the holy fathers—that which at Nicaea was delivered with authority to the holy church of God— spotless and unimpaired unto the end."

21. I do not know that this place has been identified.

22. Died 454, three years after his deposition at Chalcedon.

23. For the explanation of these words, see below, page 133.

24. *Note to the 2009 edition*: The Syriac text and the notes associated with it have been omitted here. See note 4.

25. See Hallier, *Untersuchungen über die edessenische Chronik* p. 76; and cf. Harnack, *Dogmengeschichte*,[3] ii. p. 367, bottom.

26. He appears to have been the first formally to impeach the orthodoxy of Eutyches.

27. See the epistle of Nonnus of Edessa, written to the Emperor Leo, and signed by a number of the bishops of the region (Assemani, *Bibl. Or.*, i. 258).

28. Cyril of Scythopolis was no ordinary biographer, but a zealous and trustworthy historian, careful of his statements and critical of his sources. For his Life of Euthymius, moreover, he had especially good material at his disposal.

29. Hallier, *Untersuchungen über die edessenische Chronik*, p. 115 f.; Syriac text, p. 152.

30. According to Theophanes Confessor (ed. Classen, i. 170, 172), Leo wrote the letters two years after his accession. Similarly Georgius Cedrenus (Migne, col. 662), "tertio anno."

31. As, e.g., Harnack is inclined to believe (*Dogmengeschichte,³* ii. 342, note 1). For the contrary view, see Neander's *History of the Church*, (trans. Torrey), ii. 528 f.

32. There would be nothing strange, to be sure, in Simeon's writing to the patriarch John at this time, urging him to keep clear of Nestorius and his doctrines. We have a letter of Theodosius to the Stylite, written shortly before the convening of the council, in which the emperor beseeches him to use his influence with John of Antioch to this end (Harduin, *Acta Conciliorum*, i. 1685). It was, perhaps, with that letter in mind that this one was composed.

33. This collated copy of the Syriac text was very kindly made for me, at my request, by the Rev. G. Margoliouth, of the British Museum. *Note to the 2009 edition*: The Syriac text and the notes associated with it have been omitted here. See note 4.

34. B adds, "the accursed " (plural).

35. "Das Fälschen von Acten war im 5.–7. Jahrhundert eine wichtige Waffe zur Vertheidigung des Heiligen" (Harnack, *Dogmengeschichte,³* ii. 371, note 4).

36. The silence of the *Life* on Simeon's doctrinal views (due perhaps to the fact that its authors did not fully sympathize with him in this regard) would also have assisted materially.

37. Evagrius (*Eccl. Hist.*, p. 20) narrates how he once was permitted to see the body of the great Stylite; which, it seems, was not quite safe from relic-hunters. The face was well preserved, he writes, "excepting such of his teeth as had been violently removed by faithful men."

38. *Note to the 2009 edition:* The untranslated Syriac text from Torrey's original article has been omitted here and Rev. Lent's translation of the colophon inserted instead. See page xvii of the present volume for further discussion.

39. See the numerous examples in Payne-Smith.

40. It may be that we have his words in the last section of the colophon, where, after the two authors of the work have made their request the prayers of the reader, the scribe adds his own request.

GENERAL INDEX

Also available in the Christian Roman Empire Series

The Life of Belisarius
    by Lord Mahon (1848)

The Gothic History of Jordanes
    Translated by Charles Christopher Mierow (1915)

The Book of the Popes (Liber Pontificalis)
    Translated by Louise Ropes Loomis (1916)

The Chronicle of John, Bishop of Nikiu
    Translated by R. H. Charles (1916)

The Ecclesiastical Annals of Evagrius:
A History of the Church from AD 431 to AD 594
    by Edward Walford (1846)

The Life of Saint Augustine: A Translation of the
Sancti Augustini Vita by Possidius, Bishop of Calama
    by Herbert T. Weiskotten (1919)

For more information on this series, see our website at:
http://www.evolpub.com/CRE/CREseries.html

www.ingramcontent.com/pod-product-compliance
Lightning Source LLC
Chambersburg PA
CBHW022023090426
42739CB00006BA/264